# Method Acting and
# Its Discontents

# Method Acting and Its Discontents

## On American Psycho-Drama

✦

Shonni Enelow

NORTHWESTERN UNIVERSITY PRESS
EVANSTON, ILLINOIS

Northwestern University Press
www.nupress.northwestern.edu

An earlier version of the text of chapter 3, "The Method and the Means,"
appeared in *Theatre Survey* in April 2012.

Printed in the United States of America

10  9  8  7  6  5  4  3  2  1

Library of Congress Cataloging-in-Publication Data

Enelow, Shonni.
    Method acting and its discontents : on American psycho-drama / Shonni
Enelow.
        pages cm
    Includes bibliographical references and index.
    ISBN 978-0-8101-3140-8 (cloth : alk. paper) — ISBN 978-0-8101-3141-5
(e-book) — ISBN 978-0-8101-3183-5 (pbk. : alk. paper)
    1. Method acting—Psychological aspects. 2. Method acting—Political
aspects. 3. American drama—20th century.  I. Title.
    PN2062.E54 2015
    792.02'8—dc23
                                                              2015004445

# CONTENTS

## ACKNOWLEDGMENTS

The truism that a first book is autobiography feels almost uncomfortably appropriate in my case. The research that became this book officially began when I was a doctoral student in Comparative Literature at the University of Pennsylvania, but in some ways launched quite a few years earlier, when I arrived at New York University's Tisch School of the Arts for a conservatory-style BFA in Theater. I thought of my acting and directing classes at Tisch (where I was a student at Playwrights Horizons Theater School) many times while writing these chapters, recalling (sometimes with a blush) my monologues and scene work, my classmates and teachers, and the general panic and exhilaration of theater training. While at Tisch, in addition to my classes, I was very fortunate to work with an outstanding group of artists on two research theater projects led by the radiant thinkers Una Chaudhuri and Fritz Ertl, who taught me to think rigorously about theater and to use theater for thinking rigorously. I would never have pursued academia had I not encountered two extraordinary scholars at NYU, Una Chaudhuri (again) and Emily Apter; for their brilliance and generosity, I will always be grateful.

I had exceptional mentorship in graduate school at Penn, and I thank Jean-Michel Rabaté and David Kazanjian for their kind, perceptive, and fortifying guidance, and Charles Bernstein, my advisor and committee chair, whose humor, enthusiasm, and incisive understanding helped me navigate many rough waters. The first inklings of this book emerged from a seminar with Amy Kaplan and a tutorial with Gerald Prince, and I am grateful for their encouragement at those early stages. I am also grateful for the warm and committed support of Kevin Platt in the Comparative Literature Program, as well as for his friendship.

Many thanks are also due to the librarians and archivists at the Harvard Theater Collection at Houghton Library, the Wesleyan Cinema Archive, and the Wisconsin Historical Society's Theater and Performance Collection. The final stage of research for this book was made possible through the support of a faculty fellowship at Fordham University. My colleagues in the English Department at Fordham, especially Sarah Zimmerman, Anne Fernald, and Stuart Sherman, gave me much-appreciated support at crucial times. The wit and infectious intellectual energy of Keri Walsh have contributed much joy to the final stages of this research. I also thank the participants in "Rethinking Realist Acting," the symposium Keri and I organized with Mary Luckhurst at Fordham in 2014, for their stimulating scholarship and conversation.

I am grateful to have had the editorial support of Michael Levine at Northwestern University Press, and I thank all those at Northwestern who helped guide the book through the publication process. Many colleagues read and commented on chapters and sections of this book in various forms: the members of the Modernist and Twentieth-Century Studies Group at Penn, the anonymous readers who commented on an early form of the Baldwin chapter for *Theatre Survey*, the Mellon Summer School for Theater and Performance dissertation writing workshop led by Katherine Biers, the Dramaturgies of Crisis seminar at the American Comparative Literature Association conference of 2012, the New York City Americanist Writing Group led by Jennie Kassanoff, and Keri Walsh. Isabel Geathers and Sarah Enelow gave me critical help with editing, and Meg Taylor generously provided much-needed publishing advice. I count myself very lucky to have found a cohort of junior theater scholars whose friendship and colleagueship have sustained me in the last several years in both intellectual and emotional ways: Jacob Gallagher-Ross, Miriam Felton-Dansky, Christopher Grobe, and Julia Jarcho. Martin Harries also deserves special mention for his inspiring scholarship and pedagogy as well as his generous advice throughout this publication process. About Una Chaudhuri (again!), what can I say? She is the definition of indispensable: an unparalleled mentor, collaborator, intellectual (and personal) role model, and friend.

Over the past ten years, I've worked intimately, as a dramaturge, playwright, and occasional performer, with two remarkable theater directors on a series of artistic projects that fed my research in both direct and indirect ways. My collaborations with Josh Hoglund, treasured artistic ally and friend, have taught me so much about theater (and life in general). In the last several years, my work with Katherine Brook (especially our production of Tennessee Williams's *Suddenly Last Summer* and our new work, *The Power of Emotion*) has contributed directly to my ideas about gender, emotion, and acting. My creative and intellectual life would be much less rich and rewarding without our deeply engaged and thoroughly dialogic collaboration and friendship.

Lastly, I thank my family and close friends for their vital support and encouragement. Kathleen Miller, Kate Blumm, and Katherine Brook read drafts, helped with editing, cheered me at low moments, and inspirited me with their vibrancy and wisdom. My brother Noah, whose intellectual and ethical commitments have always been a model to me, has been an enthusiastic and unwavering supporter. This book is dedicated to my wonderful parents, Deborah and David Enelow, who have taught me so much about the pleasures and values of reading and thinking, and whose joy in living causes me such admiration and delight. It is also dedicated to Michael Garofalo, my spouse and partner, whose intelligence, humility, and compassion constantly move and inspire me.

# Method Acting and
# Its Discontents

# INTRODUCTION

In 2013, for the traditional evening of comedy at the White House Correspondents Dinner, the office of Barack Obama contributed a parody video starring Steven Spielberg, Tracy Morgan, and Obama himself. The conceit of the video was that Spielberg's next film, following his celebrated *Lincoln*, would be called *Obama*, and that, after much thought, the director realized he had the perfect person to play the current president:

> SPIELBERG: Daniel Day-Lewis! He *becomes* his characters. Hawkeye, from *Last of the Mohicans*, Bill the Butcher, from *Gangs of New York*, and Abraham Lincoln, in *Lincoln*. And you know what, he nailed it.

> (*The video cuts to Obama, sitting in his office, half of which has been converted into a sound stage, with the title "Daniel Day-Lewis" and the subtitle "METHOD ACTOR."*)

> OBAMA: Was it hard playing Obama? I'll be honest—yeah, it was. This accent . . . took a while.

> (*Cut to Obama practicing catch-phrases in a mirror: "Look." "I love you back!"*)

> The cosmetics were challenging. . . . I mean, you wouldn't believe how long it takes to put these ears on in the morning. . . . I don't know how he walks around with these things.

> SPIELBERG: But once we had Daniel to play Obama, we had to cast the rest of his team. And I think we've got some pretty terrific performances.

> (*Cut to actor/comedian Tracy Morgan, with the title "Tracy Morgan" and the subtitle "ACTOR."*)

> MORGAN: Working with a legend like Daniel is intimidating. But he makes everyone better. Without him, I never could have played Joe Biden. Literally. "Hi, I'm Joe Biden."

> (*Morgan looks around sheepishly. Cut back to Obama.*)

> OBAMA: The hardest part? Trying to understand his motivations.[1]

Everybody, it seems, knows enough about Method acting to participate in the video's humor, with the combination of irony and incredulity that accompanies so many references to Method acting in popular culture.[2] But our familiarity with the trope of Method acting shouldn't stop us from marveling at the strangeness of it. How does a technique, a way of working in a particular art form, become a seemingly universally apprehended feature of our cultural landscape, held in common wonderment, adulation, and, perhaps, contempt? Why did an acting technique developed by a small number of New Yorkers in the 1930s, '40s, and '50s, based on the theories of Russian theater director Constantin Stanislavsky and associated in particular with Lee Strasberg, not only enter public discourse and endure there for almost a century, but moreover come to figure such potent cultural concerns as this video evokes? These are some of the questions that led to the writing of this book, which attempts to follow two tracks simultaneously: the actual practices of Method acting and the artists engaged with it, and its discursive history as a cultural fetish, slogan, and joke. "Rarely has a culture been riveted for so long about the technical aspects of an art," Stanislavsky scholar Sharon Marie Carnicke has remarked, but the Obama video, with its striking ventilation of some oft-repressed national obsessions, fears, and desires, demonstrates the ways that Method acting as a cultural figure exceeds the bounds of its "technical aspects."[3] The idea of Method acting is far more complicated, and formidable, than the sum of its technical parts.

After all, this is a video about race and the performance of American politics, one that conjures centuries-old questions about American identity. Method acting, Spielberg's prologue implies, has allowed Day-Lewis to become so many different kinds of Americans, in his "Hall of Human Origins"–style march through American history (with the British actor as the precolonial template): an adopted/assimilated Indian from the revolutionary period, a mid-nineteenth-century New York gangster, the Civil War president—so why not Obama? The inclusion of Tracy Morgan drives the point home: of course, no one would ever accept Morgan as Joe Biden. As depicted here, although Method acting permits an actor to cross eras, classes, even ethnicities, its universalism has at least one inviolable boundary. Indeed, the specter of blackface haunts the video, although the cosmetics it allows are only of the auricular kind.[4] Ironically, its comedic conceit—that Day-Lewis *does* become Obama—mocks not only Method acting and our faith in its uncanny power, not only the cultural history that forecloses the possibility of innocent cross-racial performance, but also the not-so-hidden belief that Obama is just a smooth pretender: that he is actually an actor, pretending to be our president, and an only intermittently convincing one at that. On the one hand, he's implausible as a Lincoln follow-up because he's not performing up to snuff (he doesn't look or act like the other presidents); on the other, he's inauthentic because he *is* performing—because he acts *too* much *like* a president. Here Method acting stands for a certain conception of acting as "becoming" (as in "Day-Lewis becomes his characters"), the total merger of actor and character, inciting both our discomfort around the possibility of inauthenticity, a disjuncture between the performed person and the real person, and our perhaps more primary fear of the opposite—of the total unity between the two. This is the anxiety that piques the comedic layering of the Method actor and the president: the possibility that we wouldn't be able to tell the difference. In fact, Method acting has figured this possibility more than once during Obama's presidency: in 2010, White House press secretary Robert Gibbs responded to the criticism that the president was not being emotive enough about the BP oil spill by remarking that Obama "believes this crisis will be solved by plugging the hole and responding to the damage done, not by method acting."[5] In a striking reversal of its original aims, here Method acting becomes a symbol of the theatricality that is opposed to real speech and action; it is as if the proximity between "mere" acting and "real" feeling, on which the Method relies, requires its expurgation in an antitheatrical defense of Obama's plain speaking.

Since its popularization after the Second World War, the idea of Method acting has absorbed and directed a complexly interrelated set of anxieties. In the midcentury, the primary subject of this book, those anxieties tended to center around the impact of psychoanalysis and the effect of ethnic and racial integration and assimilation on national identity, the latter still visible in the Obama video. For this reason, I don't think you can analyze Method acting without examining its fate in cultural discourses beyond those of theater and film. No method is neutral: all methods—disciplinary methods, technical methods, hermeneutic methods—have histories, are connected to cultural practices, and depend on axiomatic ideologies. The technical aspects of acting are even more directly linked to their histories and ideologies than those of other art forms: as one theater scholar has put it, "Acting styles reflect, enforce, and critique cultural modes of behavior."[6] Indeed, although many if not all works of performance studies therefore draw from cultural studies in some way, a book on Method acting is in a unique position to do so, because of its unusual career in twentieth-century (and now twenty-first-century) popular culture.

But Method acting is a difficult subject to write about, both because of its double history as an actual artistic practice and a generalized and inexact, but nonetheless vivid, figure in the cultural imaginary, and because of the long-standing suspicion that surrounds its study, from partisans as well as detractors. My subtitle primarily refers to psychological drama, the kind of dramatic literature most associated with Method acting, but it also points to the psychodrama of Method acting itself: the controversies and hostilities, allegiances and schisms that characterize its obstreperous history. This is a drama—the drama of the Method—that has not yet been fully played out on the scholarly stage. It is the context for the smirks and sighs that accompany many references to Method acting, as well as for the numerous popular, student-driven books that either prop it up or tear it down. Method acting, and Lee Strasberg himself, make people mad.[7] This may be one reason that, despite a recent resurgence of interest in Stanislavsky, Strasberg's Method acting has been much less studied. Another reason may be uncertainty about Method acting's status as an object of inquiry: Is Method acting a bastardization of Stanislavsky? A loosely knit practice, less theoretical than cultish, sustained by a burgeoning celebrity culture and some good gossip and publicity? A Cold War nationalist embarrassment? All of the above? And does the fact that Method acting means something so different in common parlance today from what it did in the midcentury suggest a meaningful transformation of its content, or simply reveal its emptiness as a signifier?

I am less interested in finding definitive answers to these questions and more interested in investigating what is behind them: Why do we suspect Method acting to be a fake, a cult, a tool of nationalist propaganda? Why has Method acting incited such suspicion and such anxiety? David Krasner describes the hatred of Strasberg as almost pathological: "Assailing Strasberg has become a favorite pastime, particularly for many with a rhetorical ax to grind and few facts on which to grind it."[8] However, one cause of intellectual skepticism has surely been the important and persuasive feminist critiques of Method acting in the 1980s and 1990s, from Sue-Ellen Case and others, who argued that Method acting's techniques and practices were inherently sexist.[9] J. Ellen Gainor has recently asserted that the rejection of Stanislavsky-based acting should be seen in context of the "power matrix" of male Method playwrights, directors, and actors who dominated theater for most of the twentieth century: because realist plays, Method-influenced directors, and Method actors seemed so inextricably linked by the 1980s, Gainor argues, many feminists thought the only way out was to reject the whole thing.[10] I would also argue that another, less obvious, reason that Method acting has not been the object of sustained analysis in contemporary scholarship has to do with the history of performance studies as an academic discipline, which emerged exactly at the moment that Method acting fell out of favor. The shift in performance studies away from what Richard Schechner called the "drama-script dyad," on which "we in the west are accustomed to concentrating our attention," and toward the "theater-performance dyad," the focus of "the avant-garde in the west, and traditional theaters everywhere," was part of a movement away from Method acting and the kind of theater that, by the late 1960s, it represented.[11]

This book offers a theory of Method acting as it both reflected and affected aesthetic and political concerns during the late 1950s and early 1960s, just before this shift, as Method acting was reaching a crisis.[12] One way it crafts this theory is by reexamining a few dramatic texts from that period that offer a different view of Method acting than the one we are accustomed to. Polemics about Method acting are plentiful; the current study is not one of them. Instead, to borrow terms from Eve Sedgwick, I try to balance a "paranoid reading" (ideology critique, hermeneutics of suspicion) with a "reparative reading," taking pleasure in discovering hidden or forgotten vectors of investments and desires that course through Method acting's history.[13]

## A Short History

This is neither a book about Stanislavsky nor a history of Stanislavsky's influence on acting training in the United States. Unlike most scholars who approach Method acting, I am interested in the nearness or distance of Strasberg from Stanislavsky only if it can help me illuminate something about the former. Nonetheless, the basic history of Stanislavsky's theories and practices and their reception in the United States is worth rehearsing briefly as background.

Constantin Stanislavsky, one of the major innovators of twentieth-century theater, and the one with the broadest influence in the United States, developed his theatrical theories and practices as an actor and then as a director at the Moscow Art Theater (MAT), which he founded with Vladimir Nemirovich-Danchenko in 1898. At the MAT, Stanislavsky experimented with a naturalistic theatrical style, instructing actors to ignore the audience and attempting to inspire their belief in the actuality of the scene with realistic design effects.[14] Crucially, what Stanislavsky developed at the MAT over the next three decades was "both an aesthetic model . . . and a set of teachable techniques," as well as what William Worthen has called "an ethos for the actor."[15] Carnicke argues that Stanislavsky's acting techniques, which evolved substantially over time (and which he insisted were not only applicable to realist and natu-ralist drama), all worked together for the overall goal of increasing the actor's capacity for on-stage "experiencing," a term with such a singular definition for Stanislavsky, who adapted it from Tolstoy, that one Russian dictionary designates a separate meaning: "the genuine penetration of a psychic state in a represented character."[16] Stanislavsky devised what he called an art of "experiencing," which he opposed to those of "crafts-manship" and "representation," which he thought characterized earlier forms of acting.[17] The exercises and techniques he developed to increase the actor's capacity for on-stage "experiencing" included close study of the script and various methods of interpreting it, exercises to develop the actor's imagination and psychological awareness, and physical training.

Stanislavsky drew from diverse sources, and many of his ideas are pre-figured in the work of previous theatrical theories, most importantly Denis Diderot's *Paradox of the Actor*, which crucially influenced nineteenth-century acting theory, and the theories of G. H. Lewes, who Joseph Roach has argued was the first to expound many of the foundational ideas of modern acting. Lewes, himself an actor, drew from his own experience as well as scientific knowledge in physiology and psychology in *The Physiology of Common Life*, which took an integrated view of mind and body, the actor's internal state and his or her physical expressiveness.[18] Stanislavsky also drew from contemporary directors like Duke George Saxe-Meiningen in Germany and André Antoine in Paris, and his ideas paralleled developments in drama as well.[19] Outside theater theory, Stan-islavsky's influences were also diverse: he drew from the memory theories of Théodule Ribot, the founder of French *psychologie nouvelle*, and from Ivan Pavlov's theories of reflex and conditioning, as well as Tolstoy's aes-thetic theory and the philosophy of yoga. Stanislavsky's effort to articulate a systematic method of actor training and especially of rehearsal, however, what he called "a grammar of acting," was something quite new.

Because Stanislavsky developed his ideas through long-term experi-mentation and did not publish an explanation of his practices and theories until three decades into his work (and even then, as Carnicke notes, "all his texts are works in progress"), those influenced by Stanislavsky, even his own students, were typically aware of only some of his ideas.[20] As a result, his influence was diverse and even contradictory, both in Russia and in the United States, where his ideas took hold in the mid-1920s, after the MAT's famous tour of East Coast cities in 1923–24. Its style of per-formance became a sensation in the United States: as Carnicke describes, American audiences applauded "the actors' seamless portrayal of charac-ter, their creation of an illusion of real life without obvious theatricality but with clear artistry, and their ensemble work."[21] Another commentator she cites focuses on the MAT actors' "credibility." The success of the U.S. tours led Stanislavsky to give Richard Boleslavsky, a founding member of the First Studio, permission to lecture and publish about their work.[22] Soon after, he founded the American Laboratory Theatre with another former MAT member, Maria Ouspenskaya, where they taught their own versions of the First Studio's techniques and, in 1933, Boleslavsky published *Acting: The First Six Lessons*, the first book published in the United States to lay out theories and exercises based on the work of the MAT.

Boleslavsky's book, which I analyze in my first chapter, adapted Stanislavsky's ideas in crucial ways and laid the foundation for American Method acting's specific trajectory. Two of Boleslavsky and Ouspenskaya's young students at the Lab, Lee Strasberg and Harold Clurman, both of whom were disenchanted with commercial American theater and American modernist "little theater," joined Cheryl Crawford in 1931 to start the Group Theatre, an ensemble company that would put what they learned from the Lab into practice and create an ensemble theater like the MAT's, performing plays of social and political relevance.[23] Strasberg was in charge of training the actors, and he used his own version of the techniques he had learned from Boleslavsky, emphasizing internal techniques like emotional memory, which formed the basis of what came to be known as Method acting. Other methods also came out of the Group Theatre, however. The most famous was from Stella Adler, who, dissatisfied with Strasberg's approach, visited Stanislavsky in Paris and reported back that, contra Strasberg's interpretation, the system was properly based on physical actions instead of emotion and psychology.[24] There is much debate about how to read this "correction." Rose Whyman argues that Stanislavsky was under pressure from the Soviet authorities to downplay the psychology in his system, which they deemed bourgeois; Carnicke convincingly argues that the official state genre of socialist realism fixed Stanislavsky in a realist model that he otherwise would have left behind.[25] What is clear is that the Stanislavsky represented in the United States by Boleslavsky and by Elizabeth Reynolds Hapgood's first English translation of his writings presents only a limited view.[26]

The term "Method acting" has been used critically to refer to all American Stanislavsky-based acting; Rosemary Malague's recent book, *An Actress Prepares: Women and "the Method,"* for instance, analyzes Adler, Uta Hagen, and Sanford Meisner as well as Strasberg under the rubric of "the Method." All of these teachers had their own unique takes on Stanislavsky and developed their own training exercises, rehearsal practices, and ideas about the work of the actor, sometimes described as "Method acting." Adler, Strasberg's foremost rival, whose techniques, along with Meisner's, represent the most influential American alternatives to Strasberg, emphasized knowledge of the play's "given circumstances" (a term invented by Stanislavsky to refer to everything the play tells the actor about the characters and their situation) and focused on imagination, historical research, and character action; she rejected the use of the actor's own personal memories and emotions.[27] Meisner, whose repetition exercise has become de rigueur in many acting schools, based his techniques on what he called "the reality of doing," training actors in real observation, real listening, and real reacting on stage, teaching them to follow their instincts and focus not on themselves but on what's around them; his famous formulation for this interactive, impulse-based acting is "the pinch and the ouch."[28] In this book, however, my focus is restricted to Strasberg, and even more specifically to Strasberg's work at the Actors Studio in the late 1950s and early 1960s.

Strasberg was not part of the founding of the Actors Studio, by his former Group Theatre colleagues Elia Kazan, Robert Lewis, and Cheryl Crawford in 1947, but by the period of my examination, he had become synonymous with it. The Studio, which the founders had started to strengthen American acting and to give unemployed actors something to do with their time, had become an object of fascination, both for its membership of stage and screen stars and also for its famously hermetic disposition under Strasberg, who became its artistic director in 1951. It was also famous (and infamous) for the particular qualities of Strasberg's instruction, which continued in the vein he had begun at the Group Theatre, emphasizing emotional and personal truth. In fact, Strasberg repeatedly asserted he drew more from Stanislavsky's pupil and collaborator Evgeni Vakhtangov, whom Stanislavsky asked to run the First Studio in 1916, than from Stanislavsky himself. Vakhtangov was integral in the development of Stanislavsky's psycho-technique, which he also adapted along the lines of his own taste and interest. Vakhtangov's productions were known for their emotional intensity and nonrealist stylization. Importantly, he modified Stanislavsky's "magic if" (in which the actor imagines herself in the same circumstances as her character), maintaining that in expressing the emotions of her character, the actor necessarily uses her own emotions. Strasberg also acknowledged that he drew substantially from Boleslavsky and his work at the Lab. But, although his way of articulating this could be confusing (he sometimes used the term "Method" to describe Stanislavsky and Vakhtangov), Strasberg also asserted that his Method, though influenced by Stanislavsky and by Vakhtangov, was his own creation. In the tape-recorded sessions of the Acting Unit at the

Actors Studio in the late 1950s, Strasberg does refer to Stanislavsky, Vakhtangov, and Boleslavsky, as well as the Group Theatre, but more often cites his own experience and the work that had been done in the Unit itself.[29] Both because of the important differences between Strasberg and his predecessors, and because the American cultural phenomenon of Method acting is due primarily to the fame and infamy of the Actors Studio and Strasberg himself, it is worthwhile to examine Strasberg's work at the Actors Studio on its own terms. The wager of my project is that we can learn something by putting these specific theories into conversation with their broader discursive functions; to do so requires (borrowing the vocabulary of theater lighting) both a spotlight and practicals.

## Methods of Reading

This book argues that Method acting and its metaphors can illuminate some of the key cultural and aesthetic issues of an important juncture in American history. It has another equally important goal, however: to rethink the drama of this transitional era by rethinking the relationship between the dramatic texts it produced and the performance practices that vivified them. Inasmuch as the late 1950s and early 1960s in theater and performance studies are most often associated with the rise of non-dramatic performance and the early development of what Hans-Thies Lehmann has famously theorized as "post-dramatic theatre," my move to reconsider the era's dramatic writing may appear quixotically conservative.[30] But it is precisely because drama was under pressure, especially from the group of American artists collectively referred to as "the 1960s avant-garde," that this period is a good place to look for the agonisms that interest me. Method acting's contradictions reveal many of the pressures that led to a transformation in American theater: changing views of psychology and inner life, the challenge of racial and sexual difference to American universalism, and a developing resistance to mediation that included what came to be seen as the mediating qualities of the dramatic text. The connection between these three transformations, generally considered discrete phenomena with little to do with each other, is one of the subjects of this book.

Method acting's relationship to text consists of two conflicting impulses: respect for the play as a literary work to be read, analyzed, and interpreted, and a resistance to "scriptedness" as such that views words as obstacles to authentic emotional expression. Despite the common criticism that Method actors elevated their own emotions over the dramatic text and fetishized inarticulateness (in the pauses, mumbles, and extralin-guistic murmurs for which Method actors became infamous), the Method was always first of all a method of reading. This is part of what we miss if we think of it only as a series of technical exercises to train actors: as both Strasberg's teaching instructions and Kazan's directing notes demonstrate quite clearly, their Methods were also methods of interpretation. This emphasis on script interpretation and analysis originated with Stanislav-sky and went hand in hand with the modernist developments of dramatic literature, including an increased respect for the dramatic text as a work of literature and an increased deference to the playwright, by Stanislavsky as well as his descendants in the United States.[31] Just as modernist drama became more literary, and the theatrical event became more concerned with the play and the playwright (in 1968, two theater scholars put it this way: "In 1850 a playgoer would plan to see an Edwin Forrest perfor-mance, in 1900 to see a David Belasco production, and in 1950 to see a Tennessee Williams play"),[32] Stanislavskian modernist acting relied on the actor and director's capacities as a reader and writer—their abilities, that is, to read the psychological subtext of a character, a scene, and a drama (or film script), and to write those interpretations into the performance with the actor's body. However, the American Method was also subject to the counterpressures of its own cultural context. Even as it continued Stanislavsky's attention to reading and writing, Method acting evinces, in its drive toward a truth that may not be written or even writable, a desire to go beyond the text, to write *over* it, just as the famous pauses and mumblings of Method actors indicate (to fans as well as foes) that the script is not enough. In this construction, the script represents more than the play at hand; it stands for "scriptedness" in general: social rules and conventions, authoritarian directives, and repressive cultural norms, as well as the conformity that seemed to attend mass cultural production and shackled free expression.

This double-edged relationship to text traces back to the Group The-atre, which Harold Clurman started with Strasberg and Cheryl Crawford in direct opposition to the Theatre Guild, the most successful New York art theater to emerge from the 1920s. As Clurman recalls in his account of that era, his dissatisfaction with the Guild stemmed from its particu-larly commercial relation to "distinguished plays":

> Their platform, from the first, was to do distinguished plays accord-ing to the best professional standards. Their function was to bring plays previously regarded as uncommercial to a big middle-class audience. . . . It is a fact that no American theatre organization ever

brought to the boards so many worth-while scripts. But it seemed to me, after I had worked with them a while, that they had no blood relationship with the plays they dealt in. They set the plays out in the shop window for as many customers as possible to buy. They didn't want to say anything through the plays, and the plays said nothing to them.[33]

The "blood relationship" missing from the Theatre Guild's treatment of literary plays casts the ideal relation between the dramatic text and its producers as intensely, even brutally personal, familial, and tribal: the Guild treated plays as commodities, "in the shop window," while the Group—no longer a Guild, with its mercantile associations—treated them as family members. But it's a strikingly ambiguous figure: blood is both a symbol of hidden interiority (what is beneath the skin) and a powerful signifier for racial difference. Clurman's metaphor—implying both violence and vivification, simultaneously universalist and fraught with racialist significance—intimates some of the central conflicts in the Group Theatre's performance ethos as it developed and transformed into Method acting, conflicts borne out in the plays I examine in this book.

One of the book's secondary goals is to use Method acting's textual ambivalence to rethink the relationship between text and performance more generally. David Kurnick's analysis of Method acting, in the epilogue to his book on theater and the novel, demonstrates one way to approach this goal. Examining the relationship between Method acting and literary form, Kurnick argues that the Method "codified the novelization (that is, the interiorization) of the theater that had been gathering force over the previous century." He demonstrates (using the novels of James Baldwin, the subject of my second section) that the "Method's exaltation of interiority was a direct descendent of the negotiations between theater and the novel that had produced both forms' apparent ideological convergence on the issue of psychic consistency—as well as resistances to that convergence."[34] Casting a method of acting as a development of literary form opens up new possibilities for thinking about text and performance, beyond the dismissal of the primacy of text that we have inherited from Artaud and the 1960s avant-garde. My questions begin where Kurnick's leave off. If the Method actor is doing the work of the novelist, did dramatists respond by developing the resistances that Kurnick identifies? How did dramatic texts deal with Method acting's ambivalence about scripts? Moreover, what changes in the way we view Method acting if we think of it not only as a writing practice but also as a reading practice first and foremost, responding to a text's fissures and openings, in addition to its consistencies and stabilizing conventions? If Method acting is a "direct descendant" of the novel's interest in, and difficulty with, psychic consistency, how does this change the way we view the dramatic texts that transposed and negotiated that literary development in the presence of Method acting itself?

In this book, I've tried to do my own kind of "Method" readings of drama, not as a Method actor herself might read them but rather by following the traces Method acting itself has left on texts. This method of reading could be seen as an experiment in reading performance in the way that Rebecca Schneider suggests, not as the always evanescent and disappearing other to recorded or "still" arts but as a record in and of itself. Schneider asks,

> How can we account not only for the way differing media cite and incite each other but for the ways that the meaning of one form takes place in the response of another? Relatedly, how can we account for a temporal inter(in)animation by which times touch, conversations take place inter-temporally, and the live lags or drags or stills? Because the history of theatre is replete with stills, the seeming stillness of the photograph should not necessarily serve as evidence that the stilled is live no longer. To my mind, we would do well to trouble any distinction between live arts and still arts that relies on an (historically faulty) absolutist distinction between performance and remains.[35]

Schneider wants to thaw frozen oppositions between liveness and its reproducible "others," and though her primary example is the "still art" of photography, elsewhere she suggests that text is another, perhaps the earliest, "other" whose opposition to live performance should be called into question.[36] This book attends not only to the ways that texts impress themselves on performances and performances put pressures on texts, but also to the textuality of performances themselves, as readings and writings with their own narrative and poetic structures.

Strasberg's emotional memory exercise is my central example of such a counter-dramatic performance text, which enters into the plays I study in ways that both define and subvert their structures. Strasberg's emotional memory exercise, sometimes called the affective memory exercise (during the Studio sessions, Strasberg used the words interchangeably), requires the actor to recount her sensory memories of an event (the sounds she heard, what she saw in front of her, the textures she felt) and then, once Strasberg decides she is sufficiently concentrated, to stop recounting and relive the experience emotionally and physically. Of all the techniques of

Method acting, this exercise gets by far the most play in this book, not only because it is the central and most controversial exercise of Strasberg's Method, but also because it is interwoven with drama in the most interesting ways. In my readings of *Suddenly Last Summer* and *Blues for Mister Charlie*, for instance, it is emplotted at crucial, climactic moments, in which a female character both recounts and, importantly, re-experiences an emotionally heightened event from her past.

The first part of this book, "Psycho-Methods," analyzes the relationship between the exercise and psychological and psychoanalytic theory: its early connection to the study of hysteria and hypnosis, and its continued relationship to developing theories of trauma, memory, and psychic structure. I approach this connection both historically and theoretically, to argue that even though some, including Strasberg himself, took pains to distance the emotional memory exercise and the Method itself from psychoanalysis, debates within and around psychoanalysis can help us understand both this practice of the Method and the controversy that has surrounded it. The second part, "Political Methods," continues to examine Method acting's psychology but from a somewhat different perspective, focusing on the political stakes of Method acting's psychological hermeneutics. This section is not so much about theories of psychology and psychoanalysis per se as it is about how those theories were deployed in the 1950s and 1960s, and how their views intersect with a certain kind of American universalism that African American writers and thinkers were increasingly calling into question. This section also uses two plays produced in New York at approximately the same time to unravel a story about Method acting that has not been told: the importance of race and the critique of Method acting's representations of race to the larger shift away from Method acting in the 1960s. The third and final part of the book, "Methods and Scripts," uses one play and one film to connect Method acting's ambivalence about script and scriptedness to the anxiety produced by commercial acting for film and television, connecting Method acting to concerns that have usually been considered the exclusive purview of the 1960s avant-garde.

In each of my three sections, I read Method acting, its controversies, and their resonances with larger cultural concerns, through plays produced in New York between 1958 and 1966: *Suddenly Last Summer*, by Tennessee Williams; *Blues for Mister Charlie*, by James Baldwin; *The Blacks*, written by Jean Genet in French as *Les Nègres*; and *Where's Daddy?*, by William Inge. I argue that these works of drama all contain their own representations of Method acting, some explicit and some subtle, some seemingly intentional and some clearly without any intention.

I read for both structures and traces of Method acting in the works I examine: structures include the emotional memory exercise in *Suddenly Last Summer* and *Blues for Mister Charlie*, and the thematization of acting in *Where's Daddy?* and *The Blacks*; traces include the hysterical patient and the theatrically driven talking cure of *Suddenly Last Summer*, the debates over psychology and politics in *Blues for Mister Charlie* and *Where's Daddy?*, and the problem of hypnotism and bad identifications in *The Blacks*. While each of these playwrights, plays, and productions had different relationships to the practice of Method acting, each play includes commentary on performance that resonates with Method acting's ideological fault lines in revealing ways. Moreover, each of the first three (by Williams, Baldwin, and Genet), in the first two longer sections of the book, also explores, in very different ways, the relation between the theatrical and the psychic, and each challenges notions of psychological character by exploring desires, drives, fantasies, and identifications, rather than reifying the "closed" psychology and stable, unified self associated with psychological realism. What has struck me in these plays is the way their psychic landscapes actively resist containment by psychologic. My desire to estrange psychological realism is what prompted me to use the term "psycho-drama" in my subtitle: the midcentury dramas I consider are not psycho-logical so much as psycho.

In my first section, I make the case for thinking of Tennessee Williams as the playwright of the Method. Williams commented very little on the style of acting that his plays and films often showcased, but when Kazan set up the Actors Studio in 1947, the year of his breakout directorial success with *A Streetcar Named Desire*, as a "stable" for actors that he wanted to use in his plays and films, what that largely meant, practically speaking, was the development of actors he could use to direct Williams. David Savran argues that Arthur Miller is the playwright whose work exemplifies a dramaturgy of Method acting, but Tennessee Williams has an equal if not greater claim to that title: scenes from Williams's plays were used in scene studies at the Actors Studio from 1956 to 1965 much more often than Miller's were (Williams was tied with Chekhov with thirty-seven scenes used, second only to Shakespeare, while Miller was used only once).[37] Studio actors populated theater and film productions of Williams's work through the early 1960s. But just as important as this literal historical congruence is the way that Williams's plays, more than the plays of any of his contemporaries, explore the intimacy between theatricality, insanity, and desocialized desire, obsessions mirrored in Method acting and the controversies around it. As Williams remarked in his *Memoirs*, "The Actors Studio technique fitted so well my type of play."[38] One such Williams play, *Suddenly Last Summer*, is the subject of my second chapter.

The connection between Baldwin's play *Blues for Mister Charlie* and Method acting is biographically more straightforward. Baldwin was part of Kazan's Playwrights Unit at the Actors Studio; he was also Kazan's assistant on the 1959 productions of Williams's play *Sweet Bird of Youth* and Archibald MacLeish's *JB*. He wrote *Blues for Mister Charlie* specifically at Kazan's suggestion and with the Method actor in mind. But the controversial Actors Studio production profoundly affected Baldwin's thinking: afterward, he denounced both the Studio and Method acting, and in his 1968 novel, *Tell Me How Long the Train's Been Gone*, he drew a hostile satirical portrait of Strasberg. The story of this production, and its effect on Baldwin's play and his later thinking, reveal major conflicts within Method acting itself, as well as the battle between the exigencies of playwright and those of performance that had been at issue in American Stanislavsky-based acting since Boleslavsky's writings equivocated on the question of who was really in charge of a performance's meaning. Baldwin preempted this struggle by thematizing it in his play, which instructs both its actors and its audience on how and how not to read and interpret his characters; he ultimately rejects the Method's psychological hermeneutic, but not many of its foundational assumptions about identification in the theater. To tease these out, I juxtapose Baldwin's dramaturgy to one that in almost every way runs counter to Method acting's orientations and interests: the dramaturgy of Jean Genet's *The Blacks*, which opened at the St. Mark's Playhouse in 1961 and became the longest-running Off-Broadway play of the 1960s. Even though the play was directed by Gene Frankel, an early member of the Actors Studio, the play became a touchstone for the avant-garde rejection of Method acting and the kind of theater it had come to stand for. In fact, traces of this challenge to Method acting's assumptions about identity and identification are encoded in the play.

I argue in the third and final section of the book that just as film and television threw into relief the "authenticity" of theater, they also created anxiety about the status of script and scriptedness that extended to Method acting, already ambivalent about the primacy of the dramatic text. The chapter begins with an analysis of Inge's *Where's Daddy?*, a parody of the Method actor and his authenticity fetish, and concludes with an analysis of Actors Studio member and African American filmmaker William Greaves's experimental documentary *Symbiopsychotaxiplasm Take One*, which surprisingly suggests that Method acting itself contains the seeds of a complex solution to the political problem of scriptedness, one more nuanced than its aesthetic alternatives.

## Methods of Identification

The question of Method acting's psychology—its relationship to the loose Freudianism that passed for common sense and imbued domestic policy in the early Cold War era, on the one hand, and actual psychological and psychoanalytic theories and concepts that formed part of its architecture, on the other—is one of the key issues in this book. In this regard, Kazan's philosophy and practice are very different from Strasberg's; in some ways, he is the "logical" to Strasberg's "psycho." In contrast to Strasberg, both Robert Lewis and Kazan, the founders of the Studio, were less interested in emotion as such and more interested in action and objective.[39] Psychological consistency—through-line, motivation, justification—was of central importance to Kazan, whose directing practice was heavily influenced by Stanislavsky's script analysis system, but it was not so important to Strasberg, who was primarily a teacher rather than a director, and who was accordingly more interested in activating emotional expression than in molding it into a coherent, dramatic whole. Accounts of the aesthetics of breakage (as opposed to Stanislavskian and Kazanian consistency) in Strasberg's method tend to subsume those aesthetics into a different, but still logical, system: Colin Counsell, for instance, argues that the Method's iconography, which for him includes "'ease' or naturalness," "an enhanced signification of the character's 'inner life,'" "heightened emotionalism," and, especially, the "failure of expression," all speak to the Method's "logic of psychic fracture."[40] But Strasberg's apparent efforts to fix and contain emotion through methodology have another side: an incitement of performed emotion that is driven, in the Freudian sense, not by a logic of psychological objective, but by the pleasure of psychic display.

Allegations of Method acting's essentialism usually rest on its use of actors' own psyches—their memories, their feelings, their desires—which is supposed to shore up an understanding of personal identity as enclosed interior truth. But these criticisms often end up reifying the psychic containment they aim to decry. What if the use of an actor's memories instills not a sovereign subject and a coherent self but instead a temporal and psychic openness, even a foundational imitation? What if the intertwinement of the actor's memories and their performances do not fortify the truth value of emotional authenticity but rather suggest emotion's inextricability from theatricality? Or what if both directions are possible: what if the practices of Method acting signal an authentic self in some circumstances and an abyssal psychic openness in others?

I have a suspicion about the gendering of these two directions, one that is borne out in the plays at the center of this project. Here, I follow Gay

Gibson Cima's *Performing Women*, which rereads canonical works of drama for the ways in which female actors influenced and contributed to texts by male playwrights, arguing that the unique situation of the performance text, created in the moment by actors as well as orchestrated by playwrights, offers "a complex intertwining of hegemonic scripting and feminist countermovements."[41] I explore one example of this "complex intertwining" in detail in the first section of this book, but in each of the plays I examine in my first two main sections, all of which were written by canonical male writers, a female character (Catharine in *Suddenly Last Summer*, Juanita in *Blues for Mister Charlie*, and Virtue in *The Blacks*) performs in such a way as to transform the affective landscape of the work.[42] All three characters, I think, stand in for their authors' ideal actors: for Williams, an actor whose identifications reveal the porousness of the desiring body through thrilling transformations; for Baldwin and Genet, an actor who is able to strategically control her identifications and disidentifications instead of being controlled by them. These plays do not match up well with a rigid model of patriarchal realist drama, and nor do their playwrights, who were more or less open about their homosexuality. I do not think it is incidental that Williams, Baldwin, and Genet were gay, although I foreground sexuality only in my chapter on Williams. Indeed, the insights of queer theory are relevant here: one thing I argue is that Method acting can raze the boundaries between bodies and what they are supposed to feel.

As the above description suggests, identification is an important critical term in this book. It is at the center of many definitions of Method acting, including that of the *Oxford English Dictionary*, which gives one definition of "method" as "a theory and technique of acting associated with the Russian actor and director Konstantin [*sic*] Stanislavsky, in which an actor seeks *as complete a personal identification as possible with a role*, esp. by means of introspection, improvised role play, etc." (emphasis mine).[43] This description is closer to American Method acting than it is to Stanislavsky; identification is a key word in many contemporary accounts of Strasberg's Method. It is also, unfortunately, a notoriously vague concept (Fredric Jameson has called it "one of the most problematic and unexamined concepts in the arsenal of sociological cliché").[44] Even when considered in a strictly psychoanalytic vein, identification is a hazy concept: despite its centrality in Freudian psychoanalysis as a key mechanism of the psyche, what exactly identification is and how exactly it works, for Freud, is frustratingly unclear, as many scholars have noted.[45] Still, Freud's ambiguous descriptions of identification do yield relevant insights for my purpose, because what is certain is that for Freud, identification is fundamentally theatrical: a kind of psychic performance.

In the fourth chapter of *The Interpretation of Dreams*, identification emerges as an important way to describe the workings of hysteria, as "the means which enables patients to express in their symptoms the experiences of a large number of people, not just their own, to suffer as it were for a whole host of others, and to play all the roles in a drama solely out of their own personal resources."[46] Already, in this description, the metaphor is there: the hysteric's identification renders her an actor in a drama, playing roles "out of [her] own personal resources." But the analogy I want to draw is more specific. In the next paragraph, Freud explains that hysterics identify themselves with others, sometimes in dreams, sometimes in waking life, including other hysterics, whose symptoms they often "appropriate." Identification, in Freud's description, is the method hysterics use to act as if they were another, and it is crucial that this acting is an appropriation, not an imitation. In important ways, this distinction between imitation and appropriation matches the distinction between the acting techniques that dominated nineteenth-century theatrical practice and Stanislavskian acting. Identification is not just theatrical: it is the mechanism of a specific kind of modernist acting.

The association of hysteria and the identification methods of Method acting is borne out in many derisive descriptions of the Method, as I document in the first part of this book. For now I would just like to point out that attending to the slippery, fungible concept of identification allows one to see where the Method's supposed construction of individual *identity* breaks down. Diana Fuss gives a clear account of the relationship between the two:

> Identification inhabits, organizes, instantiates identity . . . Yet, at the very same time that identification sets into motion the complicated dynamic of recognition and misrecognition that brings a sense of identity into being, it also immediately calls that identity into question. The astonishing capacity of identifications to reverse and disguise themselves, to multiply and contravene each other, to disappear and reappear years later renders identity profoundly unstable and perpetually open to radical change.[47]

Identification simultaneously inaugurates identity and undoes it: the slippages of identification destabilize the identities that are created by it. It's not enough to say that Method acting *only* produces and reiterates a stable subject position—an identity—from which to identify with an other out there. At the same time as that subject position is structurally postulated by Method acting—as the seeming prerequisite for identification that is in fact a product of it—it is also destabilized, cast into doubt, and perhaps transformed.[48]

This notion of an unstable, incoherent, fungible psyche, structured and unstructured by an unruly set of identifications, matches the orientation of contemporary affect theory, which in recent years has shifted the conception of emotion away from a Romantic concept of interiority and toward a theory of relationality. Readers attuned to "the affective turn" in critical theory may notice with curiosity the shift, in the name of Method acting's central exercise, between "affective" and "emotional" memory. The distinction between the two terms, "affect" and "emotion," has been articulated in a variety of ways by different disciplines and by different individual theorists; unfortunately, the terms tend to lack specificity in both Stanislavskian translations and Strasberg's vocabulary.[49] "Emotion" gets more play in this book than "affect" does, for a few reasons, both practical (it is the word that Strasberg uses most often, especially in writing) and philosophical. In Sarah Ahmed's summation, "emotions *do things*, and they align individuals with communities—or bodily space with social space—through the very intensity of their attachments." Emotions "bind subjects together," even though they "do not positively reside in a subject or figure": they are not properties; rather, they circulate economically, "across a social as well as psychic field."[50] Furthermore, if emotion is how we name our affects and thus situate them socially and culturally into certain frames and structures, it is a more apt term for the interplay of text and performance that interests me. Emotion also registers notions of privacy, even as it cancels them, and privacy is an important idea in Method acting—a problematic ideal that, in a theatrical context, cannot, by definition, be achieved. "It is the failure of emotions to be located in a body, object, or figure," Ahmed argues, "that allows emotions to (re)produce or generate the effects that they do."[51] This seems an apt description of emotion in the theater, where emotions circulate socially in uneven and often unforeseeable ways.

## Method Addict

Method acting makes a memorable appearance in Susan Sontag's iconic "Notes on Camp" (1964), where she suggests that objects become available as camp once we detach from them enough to find their failures charming instead of tragic: "Maybe Method acting (James Dean, Rod Steiger, Warren Beatty) will seem as Camp some day as Ruby Keeler's does now . . . and maybe not."[52] Has Method acting become camp?

Perhaps; the Obama video could be evidence of it. It's fun to think that it might always have been, just a little bit, in secret—that the relationship between the serious Method and the cheeky camp might not just be one of satire—which would jibe with my project of rethinking Method acting alongside what's supposed to be opposed to it: modernism, the avant-garde, feminism, queerness. There is, moreover, an unavoidable similarity between the gaze of camp, which treats low culture with aristocratic delectation, and the gaze of any academic critic of popular culture, as Andrew Ross long ago pointed out. Both Sontag and Ross document the curious fate of cultural forms when they lose their gloss—a loss performance often demonstrates spectacularly. For Ross, this loss is camp's gain: camp resuscitates discarded or debased artifacts and imbues them with "the glamour of resurrection."[53] After all, cultural forms, even those belonging to our supposedly disposable popular culture, do not simply go away, even when we become, as Sontag puts it, "less involved with them": they decay, but they endure; zombielike, they return, with new attitudes and tones, often estranging their prior positions. Camp or no, it's time for another look at Method acting.

# Part One

✦

*Psycho-Methods*

# "She's Crazy"

A woman runs away from the camera, turns back, and screams. It is the end of John Huston's *The Misfits*, from 1961, and the actress is Marilyn Monroe. It's not a movie or a stage scream, with clean, high, operatic pitch; it's a voice-destroying, throat-splitting scream, violent and uncontrolled. Her character, Roslyn, has trailed through the movie largely in a state of distracted passivity; what has catalyzed her few bursts of action is her remarkably piquant empathy, possibly pathological (people tell her she's "nervous"). Suddenly, watching her three male companions force a group of horses into submission, she sprints into the desert. Her face is obscured, her body tenses and flails, and her scream fills the landscape. The men watch her from a distance. One of them, played by Eli Wallach, comments viciously, "She's crazy."[1]

Monroe's performance in *The Misfits* contrasts starkly to her costars'; indeed, it often feels as if she is in a different film. Although the most obvious contrast is Clark Gable, a more revealing comparison is Eli Wallach, also a Method actor, and a founding member of the Actors Studio. Wallach's performance as Guido, a bitter widower with a violent desire for Roslyn, cleanly fits into Colin Counsell's neurotic iconography of Method acting: with his twitchy physicality and perpetually furrowed brow, Wallach's Guido is undeniably alienated, an outsider even among outsiders. However, he is also pointedly scrutable and psychologically legible, revealing in dialogue, over the course of the film, the traumatic events that have caused him to be the way he is. By contrast, there is no clear through-line to Roslyn's character, no psychological explanation for her behavior; her divorce, which opens the film, appears less as a cause of her distress and more as an effect of it. Throughout the narrative, she is steered not by legible motivations or psycho-logic but rather by a series of unruly identifications—with Guido's dead wife, with the rabbits Gay threatens to kill, with Perce when he is injured during a rodeo, and finally with the horses.

That the character Roslyn was very like the actress Marilyn is a familiar assumption about the film, supported by the fact that Arthur Miller, her then-husband, wrote the script and the character of Roslyn as a "gift" for Monroe, a dramatic role that would give her the chance to be a serious actress.[2] That her performance in the film was heavily influenced by her study with Lee Strasberg at the Actors Studio is also well known: Monroe had been devoted to Method acting and the Actors Studio, where she had attended classes, as well as studied privately with Strasberg, since 1955. For the press, this was a particularly titillating development: not only was Monroe a huge star, she was also famously unstable, and she didn't just join the Actors Studio, she became obsessed with it. Her personal intimacy with the Strasbergs blurred the boundaries of pedagogy, therapy, and surrogate parenting: Monroe spent a lot of time at the Strasbergs' apartment, where the entire family was occupied with her care, and even found a psychoanalyst who worked in the Strasbergs' building.[3] Paula Strasberg started accompanying her to movie sets—including the set of *The Misfits*—to coach Marilyn on every line.[4] Strasberg had long been criticized by his colleagues for overvaluing psychology and messing with actors' psyches, but, as Shelly Frome puts it, when Strasberg took Monroe on as his protégé, "the question of therapy's place in the performing arts finally came to a head."[5] Indeed, the relationship between the Strasbergs and Monroe continues to haunt representations of Method acting. Most recently, *My Week with Marilyn*, a 2011 film by Simon Curtis, which re-creates the contentious filming of Lawrence Olivier's *The Prince and the Showgirl*, presents Method acting as a malignant distraction from Monroe's natural charisma, the artistic equivalent of her constant pill-popping.[6] As Marilyn's hovering stage mother / therapist, Paula Strasberg combines maternal aggression, psychoanalytic meddling, and Jewish parasitism: with her thick glasses and black muumuus, New York accent and Yiddish slang, she is the dark other to the bright, white world of Olivier's light comedy and Curtis's movie.[7]

The question of therapy's place in Method acting has always centered around the figure of the manipulated actress/patient, with Monroe as the paradigmatic example. In *My Week with Marilyn*, hardly a feminist film, she is the victim of Svengali-like psychological and pharmaceutical machinations; in feminist critiques of the 1980s, she is the victim of psychoanalysis's patriarchal views of her gender and sexuality. Sue-Ellen Case's influential 1988 book *Feminism and Theatre*, for instance, argues that Method acting depends on patriarchal views inherited from Freud: in Method acting, she writes, "the psychological construction of character, using techniques adapted from Stanislavski [*sic*], places the female actor within the range of systems that have oppressed her representation on stage. The techniques for the inner construction of character rely on Freudian principles, leading the female actor into that misogynist view of female sexuality."[8] Marilyn Monroe would seem to be a perfect example of the imbrication of Method acting, psychoanalysis, and patriarchal imperatives for female sexual behavior. Indeed, Rosemary Malague's *An Actress Prepares: Women and "the Method,"* which offers a feminist critique of Strasberg's methods on some of the same grounds as Case (the patriarchal relationship between the male teacher/doctor and the female actress/patient casts women's feelings as problems that need to be solved with cures that force them into submission), closes her chapter on Strasberg with the story of his relationship to Monroe under the heading "A Cautionary Tale."[9]

The goal of Malague's book is to analyze whether and, if so, how the practice of Method acting can be separated from the sexism of its history, and Strasberg is a serious obstacle: in her reading, he is the "Big Daddy" of American acting, who taught actresses to replicate his own idea of "natural" feminine behavior, broke down their resistances by severe and occasionally violent means, and confused sexist standards of commercial marketability with good acting. Malague's rigorous critique is not to be dismissed; nor, indeed, is Case's groundbreaking indictment. But I want to put pressure on the idea of Monroe and other Actors Studio actresses as passive victims of the Strasbergs' machinations, and not only because *My Week with Marilyn* makes plain this narrative's similarity to classic antisemitic figurations of conniving, parasitical Jews. One does not need to be an apologist for Strasberg to see that criticism of him and of Method acting can slip into paternalistic attitudes toward Method actresses themselves.[10] This is the slip in Bruce McConachie's otherwise useful discussion of Method acting's ideology:

> In a revealing anecdote, Carroll Baker recalled that when she and other women attended classes at the Studio, they did not wear makeup. "I mean, we were serious," said Baker. "All that was important was our studying." Like women who hung out with the beat poets, method actresses disdained the outward pretense of conformity; method actors needed no masks. Baker's ethical purity, however, prompts an important question: How could she justify putting on characterization makeup before stepping on stage to perform a role?[11]

"Like women who hung out with the beat poets"? What about women who *were* beat poets? And why not take Carroll Baker at her word—what if there really was something that some women found both intellectually stimulating and gender nonconformist about their work at the Actors Studio? Malague quotes Ben Gazzara's comment that he "really felt sorry for the girls . . . the girls [*sic*]," who "were under more pressure" from Strasberg.[12] But whenever someone waxes sentimental about "the girls . . . the girls," feminists should be suspicious.

In the following sections, I rethink the relationship between Method acting, gender, and psychoanalysis by picking up Elin Diamond's still-provocative claim that theatrical "realism is itself a form of hysteria."[13] Diamond, unpacking the relationship between Ibsen and Ibsenite realism, which Toril Moi has called the first theatrical modernism, and early theories of hysteria, the woman's illness, only comments briefly on the implications of this connection for Stanislavskian acting, instead analogizing the hysteric to the actresses of melodrama. But as I show in my next chapter, the hysteric also haunted the performance practice that developed into Method acting: the too-close, too-real, too-identified acting that has caused male commentators from Richard Boleslavsky to Guido to turn away and pronounce, "She's crazy." I then move forward in time and connect Diamond's insights directly to both the practice and the reception of Method acting in the midcentury, arguing that Method acting represents the full flowering of what Diamond saw intimated in nineteenth-century realism: that "even as realism contains and puts closure to the hysteric's symptoms, it catches her disease."[14]

Hysteria is what Stanley Kauffman, in his review of *The Misfits*, called Monroe's outburst, denying that it had any dramatic or narrative relevance; it is a charge repeated by David Savran, who argues that "the impression of hysteria is reinforced, to some extent, by the fact that the camera, for the whole sequence, is kept close to the men and far from Roslyn, who appears as a small, infantilized, out-of-control figure. In other words, the shot/reverse shot formation interpellates the (male) viewer into the action as the silent partner of the men."[15] I disagree with this reading of the distinctive cinematography of the scene, which understands it as the climax of Monroe's objectification by the camera. In fact, I would argue that it stops objectification in its tracks: in contrast to the tight close-ups of the rest of the film, in this scene, Monroe's famous face and body are obscured, ungazable, so far from the camera that we can barely make her out, while the sound of her scream is all-encompassing; it's almost as if the film itself is screaming.[16] Furthermore, another way of reading the static camera, pointed from the perspective of the audience, would be to point out the theatricality of the scene, its presentational quality. Roslyn is *performing*, which here signals neither falseness nor disempowerment. After all, out of her scream comes the key political speech act of the film: "You're only happy when you can see something die! Why don't you kill yourselves and be happy! You and your God's country. Freedom! I pity you. You're three dear, sweet, dead men!"[17]

Hysteria's ambiguous function "both to reinforce and to cancel the power of the masculinized gaze," as Savran describes this scene, gives me a way to pry open one-sided accounts of gender and Strasberg's Method, which may have tried to "contain a subjectivity grown increasingly restless and divided by carefully regulating the production of binary oppositions," but, in instances such as those that I detail in my next two chapters, was not always successful.[18] There's another story here, exemplified for me by Monroe's performance in *The Misfits*, which does not fit easily into the schema of the sovereign subject Method acting is supposed to put forth. Method acting may have attempted to construct a stable inner core of both actor and character, but its collapse of actor and character also reveals the impossibility of demarcating the boundary between the theatrical and the psychic. Method acting: she's crazy.

# Chapter 1

# "Pathological Hypnotism," Hysterical Methods

Halfway through Richard Boleslavsky's 1933 *Acting: The First Six Lessons*, the first acting manual on the Stanislavsky system to be published in the United States, a young actress confides to her private acting coach and personal mentor that she has a problem with her current role in *Hamlet*. Boleslavsky's *Acting* is written in a series of dialogues between "I" and the actress, whom Boleslavsky calls "The Creature," and over the course of the manual we see her transform from a quivering neophyte to a confident and successful performer.[1] In this scene, titled "Characterization," "I" and "The Creature" have met in the theater where she is to perform, and "I" asks her to play one of her troubling scenes for him. Boleslavsky's scene is anomalous in several ways. In all the six lessons, this is the only one in the theater, the only one in which we actually watch the Creature act a full scene. Lengthy stage directions appear throughout Boleslavsky's book, describing the action but often including "I"'s commentary and inner monologue; here, however, as "I" watches the Creature play Ophelia's climactic scene with Hamlet, those stage directions take a surprising turn. Here is a sample from the end:

"O heavenly powers, restore him!"

(*But heaven and earth are silent. The only thunder is the voice of one whom she trusted and loved. The words behind that voice are like stinging scorpions. Not a sign of understanding in them, not a sign of tenderness—not a tone of mercy. Hate, accusation, denouncement. The end of the world. Because the world for all of us is the one whom we love. When he is gone the world is gone. When the world is gone we are gone. And therefore we can be calm and empty and oblivious to everything and everyone who a minute ago was so important and powerful. The Creature is alone in her whole being. I can see it in her contracted body and wide open eyes. If there were an army of fathers behind her now, she would be alone. And only to herself*

*would she say those heartbreaking words, the last words of a sound
mind, that tries desperately to verify all that happened a second ago.
It is unbelievably painful. It is like the soul parting from the body.
The separated words crowd each other, hurry one over the other in
a fast-growing rhythm. The voice is hollow. The tears behind it are
inadequate to accompany the last farewell; the speech is like a stone
falling down, down, into a bottomless abyss.*)

"O, what a noble mind is here o'erthrown!

. . .

(*She sinks down on her knees, exhausted, staring into the blackness
of the empty house right at me, without seeing, without registering
anything. Madness next would be the inevitable and logical madness
of the mind which has lost its world.*)[2]

The Creature's performance as the archetypal madwoman of Western
theater, Ophelia, is so emotionally intense that it breaks the containment
of the stage and overwhelms her audience: watching her, the teacher feels
as deeply as she, spontaneously spouting poetic description which, if not
quite Shakespeare, is as expansive and theatrical as any soliloquy. Slip-
ping from "we" to "she" to the abstract article "the" (as in "the voice is
hollow"), he weaves in and out of identification with the Creature/Oph-
elia and is ultimately carried away by vicarious feeling.

From his breathless description, one might expect that "I" would
declare the Creature's performance a triumph. But instead he soberly
asks what her director thinks. "He says it is pathological hypnotism, not
acting," she reports, "and that I will ruin myself and my health."[3] Surprisingly, "I" agrees and tells her she needs to work on her characterization:
she must play Ophelia going mad, not go mad herself. Apparently the
Creature's performance was *too* authentic: it crossed the line from good
acting into something else—something called "pathological hypnotism,"
dangerous for her health. There is no further comment on the Creature's
performance, and no hint whatsoever as to why such a dangerous spectacle would cause the teacher to be so overtaken by poetic feeling. Are
we to be faulted if his ensuing instructions on characterization fall somewhat flat? How could the reader not be seduced, as the acting teacher
clearly was, by the show-stopping dramatic power of the young woman
on stage going mad before our eyes, "as if somebody suddenly appeared
naked in a dressed-up crowd," as the Creature's director tellingly
described it?[4]

This scenes mirrors Monroe's desert scream in *The Misfits* in compelling ways. In both, a woman's psychological breakdown is performed so convincingly that it blurs the line between the performance and what is being performed: insanity. Is the character insane, or is the actress—and if it is the actress, is her insanity a function of her performance? Or is the performance itself the insanity? In both scenes, madwomen act mad for an audience of men, who are alternately shocked, cowed, moved, and repulsed. In both cases, the male gaze is staged for the audience, seeming to offer the male subject position as the audience's own; however, also in both cases, the woman's experience takes over not only the scene but the medium itself. In *The Misfits*, the incongruity between the almost unrecognizable sight of a distant body and the cutting, overwhelmingly intimate sound of her scream almost creates the sense that the film itself is screaming. In *Acting*, as we saw, the narration is completely captivated by the Creature's performance; the narrator might as well be the Creature herself. Both scenes, as if to arrest and contain this overwhelming emotion, end with a male audience member's pseudo-clinical judgment: "She's crazy," says Guido; "pathological," says the Creature's director. Not only does each performance, Marilyn/Roslyn's and the Creature's, blur the line between acting and being, but both representations also align the actress's performance with hysteria.

That Method acting entails a form of hysteria is one of its most enduring critiques, alongside the criticism that Strasberg's techniques "resemble psychoanalysis itself—or a parody of it."[5] Both the techniques and the aesthetics of Method acting were linked to the look and feel of hysteria, neuroses, and psychic excess, and not only in representations of Strasberg's teachings but also in his sometime colleague's directing: in 1963, film critic Andrew Sarris wrote of Actors Studio cofounder Elia Kazan, "Kazan's violence has always been more excessive than expressive, more mannered than meaningful. There is an edge of hysteria even to his pauses and silences, and the thin line between passion and neurosis has been crossed time and again."[6] "Excessive," "hysterical," and full of "neurosis"—Method performances crossed the line into madness "time and again." As early as 1961, Sherman Ewing ridiculed the Method in *Theatre Arts* for implying that if an actress is playing a liar, she should "consult Freud for the motivation for that trait of character." "The analyst's couch is as out of date in the theatre as the casting couch," he concludes. "Let's send them both to the dump!"[7] The gendering of this example is revealing: like the Creature, like Marilyn/Roslyn, for Ewing the hysterical, psychoanalysis-dependent Method actor is female.

## Psycho-Method

The first part of Elin Diamond's groundbreaking *Unmaking Mimesis* tracks the female hysteric's challenge to the patriarchal systems of knowledge production in early realist drama. Diamond's book supports feminist critiques of realism, like Case's, but adds a wrinkle to them as well, suggesting the potential for a "contaminated" realist text:

> A body imitating hysteria generates other hysterias, and the solid geometry of representation, the theater of knowledge, is radically disturbed . . . It does not abandon narrative, but it refuses the closure of positivist inquiry. It does not dismantle the text as a unique source of meaning, but it destabilizes the relation between text and performance, each contaminating the other. What are the implications of a contaminated text, a realism-without-truth?[8]

Since the publication of *Unmaking Mimesis* in 1997, scholars have often followed Diamond in arguing that realism, like psychoanalysis, countered melodrama, associated with hysteria and its "ruination of truth-making," and some have extended Diamond's argument to cover Stanislavskian realist acting, but few have followed through on her suggestion that rather than rejecting hysteria wholesale, realism adopted and transformed its theatrical power both for its own ends and, perhaps, against them.[9] Shawn Kairschner, for instance, analyzing Stanislavsky's famous rehearsal process for Chekhov's *The Seagull*, argues that Stanislavsky's actors "joined hypnotized hysterics and tubercular patients in presenting performances of safely reordered and coercively reinscribed interior realities."[10] Kairschner, like other scholars, such as Jonathan Pitches, relates Stanislavsky's system for ordering and technologizing acting, turning what had been seen as mystical inspiration into scientific technique, to the psychological science for ordering and investigating what was hidden from consciousness that emerged at the same moment. But what these critics have tended to share is the conviction that realist acting "safely reordered" psychic experience.[11] Like Counsell, like Savran, they contend that this kind of acting coercively contains subjectivity by shaping interiority into legible expressions.

My reading of Method acting complicates this understanding of its coercive legibility. I want to put pressure on these theorists' versions of what Michel Foucault calls "the repressive hypothesis," reconsidering the relationship between the ordering, containing, limiting thrust of Stanislavskian acting and the luxuriating, pleasurable expressions it incites.[12] My point is not that this kind of acting is inherently liberating (which would reproduce the repressive hypothesis inversely), but rather that it exceeds its repressions. In this reading, instead of dismissing attacks on the psychoanalytic tenor of Strasberg's Method, as other scholars interested in recuperating Method acting have done, I take them seriously without replicating their pejorative tone. One of the reasons it is worth looking again at the psychoanalytic resonances of Method acting is its implications for our views of its gender politics: it's time for a new feminist reading not only of Method acting but also of denunciations like those of Ewing and of Richard Hornby, who, in his 1992 polemic against what he calls "Strasbergian acting," reports the story of an acting teacher who had sex with his female students, likening these practices to "wild" psychoanalysis. Marshaling Freud (whom he sees as a sober, intellectual antidote to such excesses) against Method acting's "parody" of psychoanalysis, Hornby's attack recalls Boleslavsky's distinction between "pathological hypnotism" and the careful, analytical work of real actor training.[13] Whereas Diamond casts the female hysteric as a powerful, disruptive, protofeminist figure, for critics like Hornby she is unambiguously a victim of male machinations, as he replicates the melodrama of female victimization at the hands of a sinister seducer. But what if the hysteric is both a powerful, disruptive figure, as Diamond claims, and also intrinsic to Method acting—not contained or clamped down by its practices, but inspired and stimulated by them?

At issue, in part, is how we understand the relation between "pathological hypnotism" and the acting training that apparently rejected it, but in fact smuggled it in, as it is smuggled into Boleslavsky's book. The relationship between theater and hypnotism has been a contentious issue since the eighteenth century, when Franz Mesmer's techniques took hold in the United States and Europe; for many Enlightenment rationalists, stage hypnotism revealed the immorality of theatrical art, as it confused the art of acting with scientific phenomena.[14] Hypnotism as a scientific technique returned at the end of the nineteenth century through Parisian neurologist Jean-Martin Charcot, one of Freud's important early influences, who pioneered the scientific study of hysteria at the Salpêtrière hospital and who found that hypnosis could induce patients to repeat symptoms of hysteria under observation. Despite Charcot's defense of the empiricism of his methods, he also made good use of the theatricality of his hypnotic techniques. His "Tuesday lessons," where he publicly demonstrated those techniques, went beyond reproducing the stages of the disorder: Charcot and his colleagues also used hypnotism to direct little plays, telling a patient, for instance, that half of her body was married to one man and half to another, and watching as two real men caressed her.[15] Georges Didi-Huberman's influential study of Salpêtrière makes the connection explicit: "The Tuesday Lectures . . . are written, or rather rewritten, just like plays, with lines, soliloquies, stage directions, asides by the hero, and so on."[16] There was also quite a bit of exchange between Salpêtrière and the commercial stage: some of Charcot's hysterics became stars in their own rights, stage hypnotists would advertise that they were following Charcot's methods, and Sarah Bernhardt, who attended the Tuesday sessions, used what she saw as material for at least one of her roles. This theatricality was a central part of Charcot's scandalous discrediting in the late 1880s, when Hippolyte Bernheim demonstrated that hypnosis was not, as Charcot had insisted, something possible only in cases of hysteria, but rather could be practiced on almost anyone. In the end, it was all just theater.[17]

Whether or not Boleslavsky intended to cite Charcot in his acting manual, Charcot's hypnotic performances of hysteria are certainly a key precursor to the "pathological hypnotism" that the Creature's director derided in her too-real Ophelia. In fact, Boleslavsky may have had a good reason for trying to distance his kind of acting from Charcot's performances. For although the spectacles of hypnotism and hysteria exemplified precisely the histrionic theater that Stanislavsky rejected, the psycho-theatrical tradition of "pathological hypnotism" was transmitted through him all the same. Stanislavsky developed the affective, or emotional, memory exercise, which would become so important to Strasberg, after reading Théodule Ribot, the French founder of psychological science who also crucially influenced Charcot's research into hypnotism and hysteria.[18] Ribot and Charcot were colleagues, and it was Ribot's theory of psychological dissociation that Charcot used to explain how hypnosis worked: how an idea from outside the body was sufficient to transform it.[19] The fact that theater occasioned this transformation is not incidental: Charcot needed Ribot's psychology to explain the workings of his theater, to explain how a psychological suggestion or dissociated idea could have real physical sway over the body.

Ribot has long been a cipher for students and critics of Stanislavsky and the Stanislavskian tradition. Eric Bentley's 1962 essay "Who Was Ribot? Or: Did Stanislavsky Know Any Psychology?" concluded that Ribot was unimportant and Stanislavsky's knowledge of psychology thin at best.[20] Rose Whyman has recently proven these conclusions wrong: Stanislavsky, who heard about Ribot while exploring an actors' training method that could help actors capture the essence of emotion in performance, read a good deal of the psychologist (his copies of his books are substantially annotated).[21] The relatively scant analyses of Ribot's impact on Stanislavsky have tended to place him squarely in the behaviorist tradition: Carnicke, for instance, locates Ribot "at the beginning of psychology as a science, and more specifically of behaviourist studies into the nature of emotion: William James and Carl Lange's psychophysical theory, Ivan Pavlov's and Ivan Sechenov's work on reflexology and conditioning."[22] Behaviorism was an important touchstone for Stanislavsky's thinking about the connection between internal stimuli and external expression, and an important element of Strasberg's thinking as well.[23] But Ribot's impact on the development of psychoanalysis is equally important, and has been much less explored. George Makari's lengthy book on the origins of psychoanalysis begins with Ribot, who, he argues, first put forward the crucial idea that psychological research required both introspection, the collection of subjective impressions, and objective analysis—all crucial theses for the development of psychoanalysis. According to Makari, Ribot thus "created a sturdy framework that organized French psychological inquiry for the next thirty years," the framework that Jean-Martin Charcot adopted around 1885, just as Freud came to Paris to begin studying with him.[24]

Ribot's writings on affective memory have much to reveal about the roots of the emotional memory exercise, as well as its connection to contemporaneous artistic experiments with memory, most obviously that of Proust.[25] What is equally important for my purposes is the light that Ribot's research sheds on the complicated relation between acting and writing. "La Memoire Affective," the pamphlet that became the eleventh chapter of *The Psychology of the Emotions* (where the term was translated into English as "emotional memory" or "emotion memory," beginning a long-standing practice of interchanging the two terms), describes the research that explicitly inspired Stanislavsky and includes a long quotation of a letter from the poet Sully Prudhomme, which strikingly presents emotional memory as a form of staging. The poet reports that when he reads a poem he wrote with great emotion in the past, he "poses" the feeling "as a model":

> It is my habit to separate myself from the verses I have written before finishing them, and to leave them for some time in the drawers of my writing-table. I even forget them sometimes, when the piece has seemed to me a failure, and it may happen to me to find them again several years after. I then re-write them; and I have the power of calling up again, with great clearness, the feeling which had suggested them. This feeling I pose, so to speak, in my inner consciousness, like

a model which I am copying by means of the palette and brush of language. This is the exact opposite of improvisation. It seems to me that at such times I am working on the recollection of an affective state.

How is this different from, say, Wordsworth's "emotion recollected in tranquility"? I think the key is staging: this "exact opposite of improvisation" is a voluntary process by which the poet's memories become fictional embodiments, staged and "posed" like models in the poet's mind. Then those copies are copied in writing. The memory is first separated from the poet, vivified and embodied by another body, "a model," and the poet *needs* this specifically theatrical re-presentation to re-present in writing: "It is indeed only this revival which could enable me to retouch the verses."[26] In other words, emotions can only be written after they have become externalized and theatricalized. This reading suggests another way of understanding the emotional memory exercise—not as rehearsal of coherent subject formation, in which emotion shores up a contained individual interior, but rather as an act of creation that makes use of theatrical material to produce an aesthetic effect. Perhaps emotional memory is not a copy of a prior original, but a return to an original copying. Memory itself is a kind of performance.

It also suggests that the equivocation around the primacy of text over performance in Method acting can be traced to an ambivalence within Ribot's original concept. It is telling that, asked to recount an instance of emotional memory, the poet describes not an original situation of writing, but a later instance of revision: this emotional memory is not a memory of an original emotional event but a memory of writing. What is the relationship between the emotion dissociated from its original circumstance and externalized in another body and its poetic transmission? Writing as a medium is incorporated in the techniques of Stanislavsky, Boleslavsky, and Strasberg in different ways, but with a common form: narration. Narration was the chosen written mode of all three theorists: Stanislavsky's account of his system is narrated by a fictional acting student, whose journals recount his experience learning Stanislavsky's acting system from a fictionalized Stanislavsky; Boleslavsky's *Acting*, while written dramatically, shifts into narration in the stage directions, which novelistically divulge "I"'s thoughts; Strasberg wrote his only account of the Method inside his own autobiography, *A Dream of Passion*, which narrates the story of his life from his childhood through his career in the theater. More importantly, narration is the method used in the emotional memory exercise to catalyze the physical embodiment of memory. In both

Stanislavsky and Boleslavsky, as well as Strasberg, the emotional memory exercise begins with narration, as the actors describe the sensory details of the memory before they are asked to emotionally experience it in the context of the written scene. Reversing the process recounted by Sully Prudhomme, they first narrate, then embody the memory. So in the second chapter of Boleslavsky's *Acting*, "Memory of Emotion," "I" asks the Creature to narrate her own emotional experience with as much detail as possible, giving him "a good journalistic account of what happened": "At first she is almost mechanical," he reports, but quickly "she starts to *be*—she starts to act."[27]

The lesson of "Memory of Emotion" precedes the Ophelia scene with which I began, in which the transference between the writing and the acting appears in full force. There, even before the Creature begins her scene, "I" finds himself transformed by the dark theater, where "my nerves begin to vibrate . . . A peculiar peace descends on my mind, as if I partially cease to exist and somebody else's soul is living in me instead of my own, I will be dead to myself, alive to the outward world, I will observe and participate in an imaginary world. I will wake up with my heart full of dreams."[28] The synthesis of the Creature's real emotional experience and the fictive experience of her character is analogous to the hypnotically induced performances of the hysteric, whose representations of her own symptoms are indistinguishable from the symptoms themselves, but the Creature isn't the only one undergoing hypnotism: "dead to myself, alive to the outward world," "someone else's soul . . . living in me instead of my own," "I" is hypnotized by the theater before the Creature is even on stage. When she "snaps out of it," he does too, offering her logical instructions; the Creature describes him as "just like an old mathematician." He counsels "organized study" and "intensive practice."[29] He also advises her to think of the author's mind, not the character's: "You don't have to think like Shakespeare, but the outward quality of your thinking must be his."[30] In other words, let the writing lead the acting, not the other way around.

Returning the authority to the author (Shakespeare, no less) is one way that Boleslavsky tries to compensate for the hypnotism that both the Creature and "I" undergo in the scene: the Author is brought in to save his own authorship from the actress's theatrical hysteria. Boleslavsky's reasons for distancing himself from the theater of hysteria were probably both philosophical and pragmatic: in the United States, the rise of the art theater movement, conceived in opposition to the commercial stage of melodrama, coincided with the embrace of psychoanalysis by American intellectuals. There was enough of a relationship between Stanislavsky's early techniques and Freud's, at least the Freud of the popular imagination, and Boleslavsky used this to his advantage.[31] But the disconnect between "I"'s internal monologue in the stage directions and his spoken commentary reveals something else, too, as the text captures what the "I" character cannot voice. Speaking one thing, and writing something else: Boleslavsky's textual unconscious allows the awe-inspiring performance to remain, encoded in his instructions to contain it. The theatricality of hysteria is both repressed in his text and spectacularly displayed by it, as "I"'s flights of rhetoric interpenetrate with the scene he is describing. They can't be kept apart; the performance lives in the writing; what makes the scene literary is also what makes it theatrical. In this scene, telling *is* experiencing; the literary work of the narrator and the theatrical work of the actor are inextricably linked.

## Lee Strasberg

> I am not talking about not knowing what one is doing. I do not mean hysteria or hypnosis or anything like that. I mean employing the unconscious or subconscious knowledge that we have, the experiences that we have stored away but which we cannot easily or quickly put our hand on by means of the conscious mind. I mean employing in acting the knowledge which functions in dreams, where we often come up with things that seem to make no sense, with things that happened many, many years ago but which we have long supposed to be forgotten.
>
> —Lee Strasberg, *Strasberg at the Actors Studio*

Not hypnosis or hysteria, but repressed, unconscious material and the knowledge of our dreams; not Charcot, in other words, but Freud. Like Freud, Strasberg retreated from public demonstration and worked privately (the Actors Studio was closed to outsiders and until the early 1960s, did not produce public performances); he contained diverse knowledge in a central authority figure; most importantly, he insisted that the true work was done in the individual mind. Like Eugene O'Neill, who also relied heavily on Freudian concepts, Strasberg denied the relation between his Method and psychoanalysis, and David Krasner, in *Method Acting Reconsidered*, repeats Strasberg's protestation that the Method is not Freudian, but Pavlovian.[32] It is true that Strasberg, with his emphasis on conditioning, imports some of the language and ideas of behaviorism. However, it is also undeniable that much of Strasberg's work at the Actors Studio, as well as some of his key theories and exercises, reproduce some of the structures and tropes of psychoanalysis: Freud's topography of the unconscious, with repressed memories that inhibit free behavior, and the talking cure, in which patients reconstruct their past experiences, leading to a cathartic breakthrough, with the goal of controlling their psychic and emotional lives. For Strasberg, as for Freud, all action referred back to psychic life; physical manifestations were secondary. Like Freud, Strasberg insisted that discharge of emotion had a powerful cathartic effect. Strasberg completed the shift that Boleslavsky had begun toward Freud: even more than Boleslavsky, his Method used the tropes of psychoanalytic discovery, and he viewed his acting students with an avowedly clinical gaze, repeatedly referring to the Actors Studio as a place for actors who were having "problems."[33] But although Strasberg's actor training was more Freudian than his predecessors'—more privacy, more analysis, less performance—his Method acting also contained traces of the ostensibly discarded theories that Strasberg, in the above quotation, registers in repression. The patient-as-actress / actress-as-patient chiasmus was sustained at the Actors Studio, where actors' psychological problems were transformed from unconscious blockage and life-impeding neurosis into valuable theatrical material.

Here is what Lola Cohen's 2010 edition of *The Lee Strasberg Notes*, which was published in cooperation with the Strasberg estate and contains the current official explanation of the Method, includes in the section on "training and exercises": first, a series of relaxation exercises, designed to release tension and "eliminate mannerisms that obscure the truth of expression"; next, a sequence of sense memory exercises, which use imaginary objects to "awaken the mind and stimulate the imagination in order to make contact with sensory memory," designed to "train the actor to re-create and re-live in his imagination any object or group of objects which when combined into a scene on stage, stimulate the desired experience called for in the performance." Actors begin the sense memory sequence by imagining their regular breakfast drink, and the experience of shaving or putting on makeup in front of a mirror, then move on to the re-creation of the feeling of sunshine; the sensation of sharp pain, sharp taste, and sharp smell; "overall sensations," which "enabl[e] the actor to discover constrictions, inhibitions, points of embarrassment, and concerns connected to the body"; and exercises using personal objects, to "explore our sensory responses to memories of a specific thing or person."[34]

Here is how Strasberg describes the overall sensation exercise in *A Dream of Passion*:

> Often an actor comes into contact with an area that may be blocked, of which he has not even been aware . . . often without any need to analyze, without any need to theorize, the actor induces sensation in that area and thus overcomes certain unconscious inhibitions or locked-up sensations. Therefore, in this exercise, we often encounter strong emotions . . . As we unblock them, a lot of sensations begin to pour through and begin to lead toward a fullness and vividness of expression.[35]

These exercises are cathartic: "locked-up" emotions are expelled in a controlled environment, resulting in greater freedom and psychic flexibility. The next exercise in the sequence is the private moment exercise, in which the actor re-creates in the classroom a scene or an action that he or she only does in private. This section includes a revealing footnote: "Once a psychiatrist called my office to ask if it might be possible for him to observe 'one of those private, obscene moments.' Private suggested to him something reprehensible or sexual . . . the exercise itself is not like that at all."[36] Distancing himself from the psychiatrist's prurient imagination, Strasberg registers the obvious similarity between his gaze and the psychiatrist's, in structure if not in intent. The anecdote also introduces a theme in the recorded Studio sessions: the exclusion of the public gaze from the private sanctuary of the Studio.

This exercise precedes Strasberg's version of the emotional memory exercise (in *A Dream of Passion*, Strasberg includes the animal exercise, in which the actor first imitates an animal, then a human with that animal's characteristics, and also the song-and-dance exercise, to free the actor physically, in between them), which Cohen describes thus: "The emotional memory exercise enables actors to access, re-create, and re-live intense past experiences from their own lives at will through the use of sense memory and the exploration of objects and people connected with those past events."[37] Actors choose a few very strong emotional memories, at least seven years old: "The experiences we choose for emotional memory work must be decisive events that have conditioned us and were influential as our highest and most moving experiences—jealousies, loves, rages, hurts, or other once-in-a-lifetime exciting or traumatic experiences." Moreover, they must be memories that have not changed over time, events "remembered even more strongly than originally experienced," because "often in the moment that it happened, you weren't able to express the feelings."[38] Although at various junctures he stressed that emotional memory was "remembered emotion, not literal emotion," more often Strasberg insisted that emotion is not only remembered, but can actually be re-experienced: instead of a remembering, the emotional memory exercise catalyzes a "re-living."[39]

Unlike Boleslavsky's, Strasberg's exercise begins with relaxation: as he explained in 1964, "We make the actor aware that things are going on within him that he's not conscious of . . . If the actor starts to relax, things lying below the surface begin to come up and truly emotional things begin to happen, released by nothing more than relaxation."[40] The body is pliant, open, and ready to let in suggestion. Once the actor is relaxed, Strasberg first guides him or her through the sensory details of the memory, and then asks about the actor's feelings. When he feels the actor is fully concentrated, Strasberg tells the actor to stop describing the memory aloud and instead to perform a simple physical task while focusing on the memory internally; now the actor should be able to fully re-experience the emotional content of the memory in the context of the scene. In A Dream of Passion, Strasberg describes a successful version of the exercise, in which an actress experiences "the full re-creation of an intense emotional experience," clearly a traumatic one, because it leads to her wailing and sobbing: "I always forget that for these exercises we need Kleenex."[41] An audio recording from the Actors Studio from 1966 captures the exercise as performed by actress Anna Stanovich; it lasts about ten minutes, and what is audible on the tape is a series of pregnant pauses punctuated by screams, sobs, and short bursts of language.[42]

The cloistered setting, the relaxation, the guiding male authority figure, the activation of the past through suggestion—the emotional memory exercise shares elements with both Charcot's hypnosis and Freud's psychoanalysis. Its goal, however, is not to cure, but to stage; not to release the actor from his or her emotion, but to activate it, over and over again, less like Freud's talking cure and more like Charcot's performances. Didi-Huberman provides one way of understanding this connection: explaining what gave hypnosis its intense theatrical power at Salpêtrière, Didi-Huberman asserts that it "made the virtual element of a representation coincide with the actual pathos of the event of a symptom." This merging of the representation and the actual—the virtual pathos and the true pathetic event—cannot help but recall the emotional memory exercise. Didi-Huberman continues,

> Or, in other words, it was the exact—I also mean exact in the sense of beyond the act—*repetition of a "first time"*; Charcot laid claim to "a

faithful reproduction" of the "local shock"—his name for the trauma in hysteria, the act. It was almost the irruption of the past act "in person," the raw, gesticulated hallucination of the act out of a simple suggestion to remember. *A theater of the return of memory*, then, like flames rekindled.[43]

This is the goal of the emotional memory exercise: to bring to life an emotion in the present through suggestion. In fact, Asti Hustvedt, in her recent account of the hysterics of Salpêtrière, intimates this connection, when she quotes Charcot's colleague Alfred Binet's description of hypnosis-induced hysteria, "in words that evoke what a century and a half later would be called method acting."[44] Strasberg offers the same reasoning for his exercise that Didi-Huberman imparts to Charcot: the emotional memory exercise solves "the central problem in acting," how an actor can truthfully express an emotion over and over again with what William Gillette famously described as "the illusion of the first time." The psychic repetition of the emotional memory exercise, designed to solve this problem, resonates both with Charcot's hypnosis and also with Freud's later theorization of trauma in *Beyond the Pleasure Principle*, which also begins with an inquiry into repetition. For Strasberg, it is necessary for theatrical repetition—the repetition of rehearsal and performance—to become a kind of controlled traumatic repetition, a return to the site of traumatic emotion on command.[45]

One thing on which critics of Strasberg all seem to agree is that trauma shouldn't be used for theater. Rosemary Malague's concern is that actors who are too emotionally vulnerable in acting class will become too dependent on the acting teacher; this is one reason she rejects Strasberg in favor of Adler: "When students are rendered dependent on their teacher to define and validate their very selves, there is an ever-present danger that they will become weak and vulnerable rather than strong."[46] Fascinatingly, this argument echoes debates around the medical use of hypnosis to cure trauma to the letter: the early twentieth-century backlash against medical hypnosis, led by Paul-Charles Dubois, held that patients should not be treated as effeminate and passive but should instead be appealed to as rational, thinking subjects. Dubois and other moral critics of hypnosis called for "the abandonment of hypnotic 'manipulation' in favor of a moral rehabilitation of the patient based on 'rational persuasion.'"[47] Similarly, debates over the use of hypnosis to treat shell shock centered on the idea that the patient would become too dependent on the hypnotist and his suggestions, and that this dependency would ruin the subject's autonomy and composure.[48]

As Ruth Leys argues in *Trauma: A Genealogy*, trauma was associated with hypnosis from the early days of the concept, not only because hypnosis provided the means to study and cure trauma, but also because the behavior of patients under hypnosis became the model for thinking about trauma victims. Leys's thesis is worth quoting at length:

> It is well known that the rise of trauma theory was associated from the start with hypnosis. Hypnosis, or hypnotic suggestion, was the means by which Charcot legitimated the concept of trauma by proposing that the hysterical crises that he suggestively induced in his patients were reproductions of traumatic scenes. What is less well understood is that hypnosis was not just an instrument of research and treatment but played a major theoretical role in the conceptualization of trauma. This is because the tendency of hypnotized persons to imitate or repeat whatever they were told to say or do provided a basic model for the traumatic experience. Trauma was defined as a situation of dissociation or "absence" from the self in which the victim unconsciously imitated, or identified with, the aggressor or traumatic scene in a condition that was likened to a state of heightened suggestibility or hypnotic trance. Trauma was therefore understood as an experience of hypnotic imitation or identification—what I call mimesis—an experience that, because it appeared to shatter the victim's cognitive-perceptual capacities, made the traumatic scene unavailable for a certain kind of recollection.[49]

The model for trauma came from the mimetic quality of hypnosis: the unconscious imitation of hypnotized subjects. This primary imitation of trauma is unavailable for a certain kind of recollection, but is available for another: for "re-living" in the trance state of hypnosis, in which the "absence from the self" allows the mimetic trauma to emerge.

Freud rejected this theory of unconscious imitation in favor of his theory of unconscious sexual desire, arguing that the hysteric's behavior had its roots in her own sexual history, not in the mimetic interplay between the subject and the "other self."[50] However, as Leys shows, the paradigm of hypnotic suggestion remained in Freud's understanding of trauma (and in fact he returned to hypnosis after the First World War to treat shell-shocked soldiers).[51] Freud came to see trauma as a function of the "originary 'invasion'" of the subject that reveals the subject's "abyssal openness" to all kinds of mimetic identifications: trauma as "the archetrauma of identification."[52] Indeed, seen through the lens of Leys's argument, criticisms of the use of trauma for acting could be understood as a repudiation of the disturbing history of the concept of trauma itself, a remnant of the mimetic theory of the psyche. This "abyssal openness" to identification denotes a disturbingly porous subject, and this porous subject, cataclysmically open to influence from without, is one way of describing the anxiety-producing figure of the actor. Is this why Method acting touched a nerve—because it put front and center "the archetrauma of identification"?

# Chapter 2

✦

# The Case of *Suddenly Last Summer*

Almost nothing happens in "Suddenly Last Summer" except that words are spoken . . . Miss Meacham plays the part with a technical virtuosity and a personal force that are hypnotic.
—Brooks Atkinson, *New York Times*, January 19, 1958

What surprises me is the degree to which both critics and audience have accepted this barrage of violence. I think I was surprised, most of all, by the acceptance and praise of *Suddenly Last Summer.* When it was done off Broadway, I thought I would be critically tarred and feathered and ridden on a fence rail out of the New York theatre, with no future haven except in translations for theatres abroad, who might mistakenly construe my work as a castigation of American morals, not understanding that I write about violence in American life only because I am not so well acquainted with the society of other countries . . . Last year I thought it might help me as a writer to undertake psychoanalysis and so I did. The analyst, being acquainted with my work and recognizing the psychic wounds expressed in it, asked me, soon after we started, "Why are you so full of hate, anger and envy?" . . . After much discussion and argument, we decided that "hate" was just a provisional term and that we would only use it till we had discovered the more precise term. But unfortunately I got restless and started hopping back and forth between the analyst's couch and some Caribbean beaches.
—Tennessee Williams, *New York Times*, March 8, 1959

"I thought I would be critically tarred and feathered and ridden on a fence rail out of the New York theatre": for the first of two times in this short essay, Tennessee Williams puts himself in the position of Sebastian

Venable, the absent center of his 1958 one-act *Suddenly Last Summer*, in a fantasy of being punished with public sexual violence for a play about witnessing sexual violence. It is also a fantasy of exile: this "future haven" abroad is an imagined vantage point "somewhere out there" temporally as well as geographically, where Williams's "barrage of violence" would be accepted as an alien artifact from an exotic culture. Williams's next rhetorical jostle is sly. He does, he admits, write about violence in American life, but "only" because it is what he knows best. He does know it, and he does write about it, but he suspects that other countries are just as bad. Still, the suggestion lingers that the theaters abroad might be, on some level, correct in their estimation, just as New York theater would have been, on some level, right to run him out of town. For Williams's "surprise" at the "acceptance and praise" of this "barrage of violence" was another sly move: concealed in self-deprecation is an insinuation that those who accept the barrage might do so because they *like* it. "But unfortunately I got restless and started hopping back and forth between the analyst's couch and some Caribbean beaches": the patient and the analyst never found the precise term, because the patient was "hopping back and forth" between analysis and the beach. It is impossible not to think of Cabeza de Lobo, the beach where Sebastian of *Suddenly Last Summer* is cannibalized by the objects of his deviant desire. Instead of saying "the word"—which he never says—Williams hops to the beach. The couch, the scene of secular confession, is scrapped for "some Caribbean beaches," the sexually free, un-American "other scene."

How might the picture of American Method acting be complicated and enriched by a serious consideration of Williams as a Method playwright? It might make us think twice about aligning Method acting with the most heteronormative tendencies of its era. It also might deepen our understanding of Method acting's relationship to hysteria. So many of Williams's female protagonists could be classified as hysterics that there is little need to name them: Blanche DuBois from *A Streetcar Named Desire* and the Princess Kosmonopolis from *Sweet Bird of Youth* are only two of the most obvious examples. As has long been part of the playwright's mythology, Williams had a biographical reason for being interested in female mental illness in the figure of his sister Rose, who was institutionalized for schizophrenia and underwent a lobotomy in 1943. Some recent Williams criticism has also revived an old reading of his female characters as masked representations of Williams himself as a gay man: that his female roles are really drag roles.[1] I want to offer another reading of Williams's female characters, their hysteria and their camp theatricality: that these roles comment and reflect on the status of acting; specifically, of "actressing." This is how I would read the campiness of these characters. All of Williams's hysterical women are also performers, if not literally actresses, like the Princess. If many of Williams's plays include representations of himself as a writer in various states of ghostliness—Tom in *The Glass Menagerie*; Allan, Blanche's dead poet husband in *Streetcar*; and Sebastian Venable in *Suddenly Last Summer*—what many of his female characters represent is the pleasure, and angst, of theatrical performance.

Marc Robinson argues that the stage-setting of one of these characters, Amanda Wingfield from *The Glass Menagerie*, represents Williams's skepticism about the stage's ability to honestly express the sentiment he longed to communicate; the melodramatic manufacturing of emotion in which Amanda is an expert, he claims, reflects poorly on Williams's own traffic in feeling.[2] If these characters reveal Williams's skepticism, however, they also reveal the cataclysmic sincerity that undergirds even our most banal delusions. Theatrical cliché, for Williams, is not something to make fun of, even if its extravagance makes us cackle; it is Williams's form of camp, a mode that Susan Sontag astutely perceived is fundamentally not satirical: "Camp taste is a kind of love, love for human nature. It relishes, rather than judges, the little triumphs and awkward intensities of 'character' . . . Camp taste identifies with what it is enjoying . . . Camp is a tender feeling."[3] Williams's tenderness toward and identification with his actresses and their usually unsuccessful performances should not be underestimated. Indeed, it is the gap between their performances of glamour and success and the "reality" that rejects them that give those performances their mock-heroic grandeur. His plays of the late 1950s, especially *Orpheus Descending* (1957) and *Suddenly Last Summer* (1958), make it clear that Williams does not believe that performances that feed off and build on themselves are opposed to "real feeling." In fact, self-conscious theatricality is often his way of representing the bottomless and formless passions that course through these plays, and, like his female characters, Williams embraces it, even as he recognizes its inevitable inadequacy.

Two such self-consciously theatrical women populate *Suddenly Last Summer*, the subject of my analysis. *Suddenly Last Summer* is not the obvious choice for an analysis of Method acting and drama; *A Streetcar Named Desire* is the play that in some ways catalyzed the founding of the Actors Studio and certainly fixed an image of Method acting in the public consciousness in Marlon Brando's inarticulate, emotionally explosive Stanley Kowalski. In fact, part of my goal in turning to *Suddenly Last Summer* is to suggest a different image for the Method actor, a female one, with a different relationship to theatricality and a different

grammar of emotion. *Suddenly Last Summer* evokes a different genealogy for Method acting, one based not on authenticity, masculinity, and
naturalness, but on "pathological hypnotism," hysteria, and femininity.

*Suddenly Last Summer* is also the play that best articulates Williams's
intertwined explorations of transgressive sexual desire, psychic dissolu-
tion, and theatrical performance, by emplotting the connection between
performance and psychiatry. Williams wrote *Suddenly Last Summer* while
undergoing psychoanalysis with Lawrence S. Kubie, the analyst with the
provisional terms that Williams declared inadequate. Williams left analysis, where, according to a letter to his mother, he had felt persecuted by
Kubie, shortly before the premiere of *Suddenly Last Summer*. Critics have
usually taken Williams at his word and painted a picture of Kubie as a
hostile and homophobic analyst (he was president of the New York Psychoanalytic Society, which took the official position that homosexuality
was a mental illness, and Williams reported that his doctor had encouraged him to stop both writing and having sex with men).[4] But it would
be a mistake to read the play simply as a critique of psychoanalysis and
its attempts to contain non-normative desire.[5] The play stages a return of
what both psychoanalysis and Method acting repressed ("I do not mean
hysteria or hypnosis or anything like that," fretted Strasberg): hypnosis
and hysteria as theatrical tools. Williams offers his own version of what
Foucault, twenty years later, would identify as *scientia sexualis*'s discursive multiplications of sexuality; in this play, moreover, what psychiatry
incites is a particular kind of narrative-theatrical act: a version of an emotional memory exercise, one that brings to the surface its amalgamation
of Freud and Charcot. In this play, narration is the contagious, irrepress-
ible theatrical act; Williams injects the talking cure (quite literally, as we
will see) with hysterical performance.

*Suddenly Last Summer* is set in the Garden District of New Orleans,
in the jungle-like garden connected to the home of a wealthy matriarch,
Mrs. Venable, who is desperate to keep her son Sebastian's reputation
unscathed by the lurid story of his death abroad, witnessed by his cousin
Catharine. Sebastian, a poet, was obsessively close to his mother, who
usually accompanied him on his summer travels but couldn't last summer
because of an illness. Although Mrs. Venable committed Catharine to a
mental hospital after the incident, Catharine refuses to keep quiet ("she
*babbles*!") about the circumstances of Sebastian's death. In order to shut
her up, Mrs. Venable tries to bribe a young psychiatrist, Dr. Cukrowicz,
to give Catharine a lobotomy, and has brought him to her home for that
purpose. Catharine's mother, Mrs. Holly, and her brother, George, have
also been brought in to put pressure on Catharine to rescind her story,

or Mrs. Venable will tie up the fortune Sebastian left them in his will. But when the doctor realizes what is going on, he insists on talking to Catharine, and instead of performing a lobotomy, he proceeds with a kind of talking cure. He gives Catharine an ambiguous injection and hypnotizes her, with the instruction to tell the whole truth. What comes out is that on Sebastian's summer travels first his mother and then Catharine "procured" men and boys for him. These were usually men of his class, but last summer, at Cabeza de Lobo, a beach in an unspecified Spanish-speaking country, he had lowered himself to the bathhouses by the public beaches and impoverished children. But more and more children began to appear, demanding payment, until one day as he and Catharine were eating lunch, an enormous mob of them came up from the beach with improvised musical instruments, and, chanting for bread, chased Sebastian to the top of a hill, where they killed him and ate him.

*Suddenly Last Summer* is based on Euripides's *Bacchae*, and like the *Bacchae*, it uses the tropes of dismemberment and cannibalism to link madness and theater. Such images are all over *Suddenly Last Summer*: the "tropical jungle" of Sebastian's garden contains "massive tree-flowers that suggest organs of a body, torn out, still glistening with undried blood," and the first flora Mrs. Venable points out to Dr. Cukrowicz is the "Venus's-flytrap."[6] Her description foreshadows what we learn about Sebastian: "It has to be kept under glass from early fall to late spring and when it went under glass, my son, Sebastian, had to provide it with fruit flies flown in at great expense from a Florida laboratory that used fruit flies for experiments in genetics."[7] Like Sebastian (whose last name, like his mother's, shares its first syllable with the plant), the flytrap goes into hibernation in the winter, and needs to be contained under glass both for its own protection and for the protection of what's around it. The expensively maintained, flagrantly luxurious flytrap, both vulnerable and voracious, is a symbol not only for Sebastian and his summer secret but also for Mrs. Venable herself, who "has light orange or pink hair and wears a lavender dress, and over her withered bosom is pinned a starfish of diamonds," another creature of this cultivated jungle of the aberrant.

When Mrs. Venable appears with the doctor, who is dressed in pure white, "glacially brilliant," like his eponymous sugar (explaining his name to Mrs. Venable, he tells her, "It's a Polish word that means sugar, so let's make it simple and call me Doctor Sugar"), it becomes clear that there are two types of character in *Suddenly Last Summer*: cannibals and their food.[8] Catharine links the Venables' money and Sebastian's sexuality to the consumption of human flesh in her first scene on stage: "Cousin Sebastian said he was famished for blonds, he was fed up with the dark ones and was famished for blonds . . . That's how he talked about people, as if they were—items on a menu." For Catharine, Sebastian's cannibalistic desires stem from a deprivation of normal nourishment: "I think because he was really nearly half-starved from living on pills and salads."[9] For Mrs. Venable, it is a sign of chastity, one that conceals incestuous intimacy: she proudly displays two pictures of Sebastian taken twenty years apart, declaring, "It takes character to refuse to grow old, Doctor—successfully to refuse to. It calls for discipline, abstention. One cocktail before dinner, not two, four, six—a single lean chop and lime juice on a salad in restaurants famed for rich dishes."[10] Her desire for Sebastian to stay a child, and under her control, is linked to his anorexic detachment from normal eating. Her comment also calls attention to the class position that makes both possible. The cannibal as a figure of deviant sexuality is a metaphor with a rich history (think of Hannibal Lecter, the cannibal dandy). It is also, of course, a colonial figure: the cannibal as the paradigmatic primitive who doesn't respect civilization and its categories. In psychoanalysis, it also figures a specific kind of identification: early on in Freud's chapter on identification in *Group Psychology and the Analysis of the Ego*, he compares identification to the oral phase "in which the object we long for and prize is assimilated by eating and is thus annihilated as such. The cannibal, as we know, remained at this standpoint."[11] All identification in Williams's play, not just Sebastian's and Mrs. Venable's, has an element of cannibalism: violent, ambivalent incorporation that expresses both love and hate, desire for the other and for the other's annihilation.

Cannibalism is also one particularly violent figure for acting, as Strasberg noted: "Without a firm, deep technique, acting becomes cannibalistic."[12] In fact, the connection between acting and cannibalistic desire comes from psychoanalysis itself: it was theorized by the second-generation Freudian Otto Fenichel in a 1946 essay titled "On Acting," which was republished in the back of the *Tulane Drama Review* in 1960, in which he reads acting as an exercise in "making test identifications," fulfilling the dependent needs of those stuck in the oral stage.[13] Fenichel's key example of such oral fixations is the case of an actress-patient who could not stop making "grimaces" while she was onstage: "In the deepest layer of the unconscious," he reflects, "they were chewing movements, and represented the impulse to devour the dismembered audience."[14] Later Fenichel adds that "her words and gestures on the stage had for her the unconscious significance of food . . . The narcissistic pleasure consisted in the fact that the playwright's 'food' had passed through the actor's personality."[15] In performance, the actress plays out her destructive desire to incorporate both the audience and the actual words of the play. Fenichel thus suggests that the cannibalism intrinsic to acting is directed not only at the audience but also at the playwriting: the actress cannibalizes her role.

It seems likely that Lawrence Kubie was familiar with this essay, originally published in the *Psychoanalytic Quarterly* in 1946, when Kubie had just taken over the Yale Department of Psychiatry. Is it possible he mentioned Fenichel's article to Williams? The correspondence is somewhat uncanny. In *Suddenly Last Summer*, performance is catalyzed by identification, which is presented as a form of cannibalistic incorporation. Each character repeats (in the narrative) and foreshadows (in the *récit*) the "dark" boys' cannibalization of Sebastian, who drives the internal performances of the two women for the doctor as well as the play itself. The competition between these two women for the stage and the doctor's sympathy is also a competition over whose identification with Sebastian is more complete: like Fenichel's actress-patient, cannibalizing her role, both Mrs. Venable and Catharine gain narcissistic pleasure from incorporating their objects and aggressively asserting that incorporation through performance. In fact, Williams's representation of the actress-cannibal goes even further than Fenichel's, to include the invisible frame of the analyst's inquiry: what incites these cannibalistic performances is the theatricality of the psychoanalytic interview.

One way to index this centrality of theater as a medium to *Suddenly Last Summer* is to watch what a different thing the play becomes on film. Williams hated it: "It horrified me, the film . . . I was so offended by the literal approach because the play was metaphorical; it was a sort of poem, I thought."[16] What he means by the "literal approach" is the mimetic representation of the play's climactic scene, in which Catharine reveals the true circumstances of Sebastian's death. In the play, what we watch is Catharine recounting and performing *her memory* of Sebastian's death. In the film, we view Sebastian's death in split-screen flashback.[17] Kevin Ohi has argued that the film uses the spectacle of Sebastian's death to absorb the spectator even as it distances her from the desire that caused it, baiting the viewer with the promise of the spectacle of gay sex alongside the promise that we will be purged of it.[18] But the theatrical medium cannot contain the spectator's gaze in the same way the camera can, and for a narrative so obsessed with theatricalizing narration itself, this changes everything. It shifts the focus from Catharine's theatrical storytelling—and her own deep identifications with Sebastian's sexual deviance—to the exotic gay male body (whose face, crucially, we never see). Furthermore, if in the film the audience gets the pleasure of containing Sebastian in a single, deviant body, in the play we get the disturbing sense that we are

always already looking at Sebastian, all over the stage. The psychoanalytic narration does not contain him, as it does in the film, but multiplies
him. George appears wearing his clothes (upsetting Mrs. Venable: "I
see you had the natural tact and good taste to come here this afternoon
outfitted from head to foot in clothes that belonged to my son!");[19] the
doctor wears all white just like Sebastian did the day he was killed (and
the doctor's medicine echoes Sebastian's pill-popping). And we are in
*his* garden, which threatens, with its hissing snakes and cawing birds, to
overwhelm us at any minute.

By George and the doctor he is dismembered (George had all his clothes
altered to fit his own body; the doctor's probing questions try desperately
to pull him apart); by Mrs. Venable and Catharine he is incorporated.
Abroad, Mrs. Venable and Catharine were substitutes for Sebastian—
now they fight over who gets to play the original. For they are not only
the twin rivals for control over Sebastian's ghostly presence, but also com-
petitors over who can perform him better. They are doubles of each other,
both structurally in the play and internally in their relation to Sebastian,
and their hatred for each other stems from their unavoidable similarity.
Each of them perform for the doctor (and for the audience of the theater), but Catharine wins: she is the better Method actor. She doesn't just
remember, as Mrs. Venable does; she relives. Mrs. Venable uses "tricks"
and artificial charms to hold her audience's attention; Catharine, in contrast, is full of "truth." So Catharine triumphs over the stage, playing out
her emotional memory not to cathartically expel but to theatricalize her
trauma, over and over again. The doctor instructs Catharine to repeat
her story—but she already has repeated her story, again and again, and
not only remembers it completely, but fully re-experiences it, and certainly "suffers from [her] reminiscences": "WHEN CAN I STOP RUNNING
DOWN THAT STEEP WHITE STREET IN CABEZA DE LOBO?"[20] The controlled
environment of the doctor's interview, like the controlled environment
of the Actors Studio, is overtaken by a traumatic memory too powerful
to be contained. Strasberg wanted to harness psychic repetition to theatrical repetition, so that theatrical repetition would stay "fresh." But in
Williams's play, the repetition itself is what wins: the overwhelming psychic repetition that would lead Freud belatedly to return to hypnosis and
to theorize the death drive, which Williams signifies by inverting what
has so often been construed as the ur-example of teleological narrative,
evolution.

In Mrs. Venable's aria near the play's opening, she describes to the
doctor how Sebastian wanted to see the Galapagos Islands after reading
Melville's description of it "looking much as the world at large might

look—after a last conflagration." They take a boat to the Encantadas, where they see that the sea turtles have laid their eggs on the sand. Sebastian insists that they return just as the eggs hatch to witness the babies running to the sea to escape the "flesh-eating birds" who, as Mrs. Venable puts it, "hovered and swooped to attack and hovered and—swooped to attack!" Instead of climbing out of the sea, like the first organisms, the sea turtles run back to the sea to avoid being eaten. But the truly perverse element in Mrs. Venable's story is not this reversal of "natural" development but Sebastian's insistence that they return to watch it. This repeated watching is the site of the death drive in Mrs. Venable's story, and why it so perversely doubles Catharine's, who watched Sebastian being eaten. When Catharine, at the close of the play, describes Sebastian's murder, it is to this scene we return: the flesh-eating birds become the ravenous children, and the "terrible savage cries" become the children's anarchic musical procession.

Williams's play demonstrates the complicity between the death drive and the figure of the queer that Lee Edelman describes in *No Future*: the queer, who figures the death drive for the social order, "embod[ies] that order's traumatic encounter with its own inescapable failure."[21] With this traumatic failure of social identity, Edelman's reading charts a path similar to Leys's mimetic-suggestion model of trauma, in which the subject's original splitting via identification is renewed through an awful experience with which one cannot help but identify. Indeed, in Freud, the homosexual figures that splitting as well: identification where there should be desire, imitation where there should be self-sufficiency. In Williams, however, this is not just the purview of the homosexual:

> CATHARINE: Doctor, my feelings are the sort of feelings that you have in a dream ...
>
> DOCTOR: Your life doesn't seem real to you?
>
> CATHARINE: Suddenly last winter I began to write my journal in the third person.

Catharine's trauma is the trauma of self-splitting, the hypnotic identification that makes her feel like she's dreaming. It is with this confession of self-evacuation that she begins recounting what happened to Sebastian—a propos of nothing except her obvious identification with him. What prompted Sebastian to bring her on his summer travels was the fallout from her own deviant sexual adventure with a married man after a Mardi Gras ball, for whom she made a public scene and became a social pariah. As she describes it, Catharine leaves the ball before her date and is escorted out by an unknown man who offers to drive her home, as her intended coupling is transgressed by an unknown, unfamiliar other. Instead of taking her home, however, he takes her to a place called the Dueling Oaks:

> I said, "What for?"—He didn't answer, just struck a match in the car to light a cigarette in the car and I looked at him in the car and I knew "what for"!—I think I got out of the car before he got out of the car, and we walked through the wet grass to the great misty oaks as if somebody was calling us for help there.[22]

The repetition in her speech—"in the car," "out of the car"—sets the stage for an act that is characterized by compulsion—"as if somebody was calling us for help there." The unnamed man may have "driven" her to the woods, but what happened next would appear to have come from a drive of Catharine's own. Or does it? Is it not rather that she is like a somnambulist, behaving without consciousness? The conversation continues:

> DOCTOR: After that?
>
> CATHARINE: I lost him.—He took me home and said an awful thing to me. "We'd better forget it," he said, "my wife's expecting a child and—"[23]

With her rapist/lover's "awful" rejection, Catharine apprehends that she has herself become a threat to the social order and the logic of reproductive futurity that underlies it. Hence the self-alienation of the third-person address in her journals: she is alienated from the identity with which she could recognize herself. She becomes another.

On November 21, 1958, just months after *Suddenly Last Summer* premiered, the members of the Actors Studio were privy to a private performance of Catharine's final monologue, presented by the actress Mary Grey during a Studio session led by Lee Strasberg.[24] Grey's performance elicited an intense response from Strasberg, captured on the tape recordings of his work at the Studio:

> I've seen good moments of acting from you . . . and yet it has never been as personal as I know you to be. And here it was personal, in a way that I had never seen it before . . . At the same time the work was worked on, simply and so on, and at the same time there were—the thing took possession of you, very well.[25]

The performance was very personal, but, as Strasberg's halting, fractured delivery (characteristic of his prolix commentaries during the Studio sessions, but striking nonetheless) articulated, "the thing took possession" as well. Like Catharine's third-person self, this thing is the written character: the split-off creation that reproaches and impels. Who is in charge here: the actress or "the thing"? Strasberg's ensuing instructions to Grey make the confusion between revelation and possession even more explicit:

> At the end of the scene where you started to talk, you then got emotional. You were not talking about it—it was just the mere fact that you were now relaxed but that you went on talking, that you had to go on talking. The talk *pulled* the impulses that were lying close to the surface . . . And it seemed to me and you said—somebody screamed—you said at some moment—somebody screamed and then you walked away.[26]

Throughout the Acting Unit sessions, Strasberg returns almost obsessively to the problem of expression and to psychic and physical blockages that impede it. Relaxation is his primary technique to remove those blockages that prevent free expression, which he refers to as the body and mind's social "conditioning." The attempt to rid the actor of blocks and repressions and release open and liberated impulses would seem to support the model of the authentic, truthful, unified self that Method acting is supposed to have put forth. But here, the actor's expression is depersonalized: "the talk *pulled* the impulses," she "had to go on talking"; the words led the emotion and the impulses, not the other way around. Like Catharine, the actress has been compelled by language she cannot control, possessed by impulses of which she is neither the owner nor the agent.

We might well say that for Strasberg, the personal *is* the possessed. It is the same in *Suddenly Last Summer*, in which the talking cure (with its revelations from within) and "pathological hypnotism" (with its suggestions from without) are all mixed up. This is dramatized in one of the play's strangest moments, when the doctor hypnotizes Catharine:

CATHARINE: Shall I start counting backwards from a hundred?

DOCTOR: Do you like counting backwards?

CATHARINE: Love it! Just love it! One hundred! Ninety-nine! Ninety-eight! Ninety-seven. Ninety-six. Ninety—five—. Oh!—I already feel it! How funny![27]

Catharine, an old pro at hysteria, knows the drill. But the fact that she knows the script doesn't make the performance any less effective. Indeed, the only real effect of this hypnotism—the only suggestion the doctor gives her is to "give me all your resistance" to the truth, as if that resistance were there and she had not been "babbling" for months—is the exposure of Catharine's desire. What happens under hypnosis is that Catharine's destabilizing sexuality literally destabilizes her body. The scene is a sexual cat-and-mouse game: Catharine insists that the doctor order her to rise, to demonstrate his power, which she does, unsteadily, which compels him to embrace her to hold her up, at which point she does indeed abandon something: "*She crushes her mouth to his violently. He tries to disengage himself. She presses her lips to his fiercely, clutching his body against her.*"[28] The play's portrayal of Catharine's own violent, cannibalistic ("she presses her lips to his fiercely") desire ensures that our experience of the story is not exhausted by our grasp of its "meaning"— the signification of Sebastian as a homosexual—if that is even what we are meant to grasp.

*Suddenly Last Summer* has been read as the ultimate expression of homophobia: a nightmarish representation of gay sex punished by the gods.[29] But the story of Sebastian's death isn't only horrifying; it's also *sexy*. Her rapid-fire, gasping monologue, interspersed with the doctor's encouraging ejaculations, most of which repeat Catharine's phrasing in a sexual duet, culminate in Sebastian "lying naked as they had been naked against a white wall." Williams presents this parody of Sebastian and the boys' sex acts less as a punishment for those acts than as a double of them—a double redoubled by their recounting. The three parallel episodes—the Encantadas, the Dueling Oaks, and Cabeza de Lobo— repeat the structure of desire and compulsion that drives the narrative of the play. Returning again to the Encantadas, getting out of the car first in the Dueling Oaks, running up the hill in Cabeza de Lobo instead of down to civilization and to safety—and, of course, returning to the site of these incidents in the psychoanalytic encounter—these events disguise their mimetic nature inside a (lurid, melodramatic, *excessive*) theatricality that only returns us to it. This is the terror and excitement of relinquishing control, which is, finally, what Sebastian represents most of all: "*He!— accepted!—all!—as—how!—things!—are!* . . . He thought it unfitting to ever take any action about anything whatsoever!—except to go on doing as something in him directed . . ."[30]

In the end, in Williams's play, the doctor's talking cure doesn't cure at all—not Catharine, not Mrs. Venable, not anyone. One of the strangest things about the play is how little is revealed in the supposedly climactic revelation. Catharine's story of Sebastian's death is what we've been waiting for all along: what Mrs. Venable, competing with Williams for dramaturgical control, has so carefully staged for the doctor and for the audience, trying to catch Catharine in a lie and reveal her narrative to be madness. But after Catharine has finished telling "her" story, Mrs. Venable maintains the line she's had from the beginning: "*Lion's View! State asylum, cut this hideous story out of her brain!*" Nor does Catharine's mother, Mrs. Holly, alter her view. Instead, she, as if speaking for us all, turns to the doctor for understanding: "Doctor, can't you say something?" she asks. Yes, Doctor, can't you give us some diagnosis, some authoritative interpretation, some *analysis*? Instead, the doctor closes the play on a disturbingly ambivalent note, musing, "[*after a while, reflectively, into space*]: I think we ought at least to consider the possibility that the girl's story could be true . . ."[31] The film version ends "happily," with Catharine released from psychiatric bondage and heterosexuality reasserted in her coupling with the doctor (although the fact that the doctor is Montgomery Clift introduces an implausibility to this pairing that Gore Vidal, one of the film's co-writers, was surely well aware of). The film's happy resolution of the analytical exorcism is commented on by another doctor, who remarks, with gruff certainty, "There's every possibility that the girl's story is true." But Williams ended the play totally differently, with no resolution except that diabolically contemplative suggestion: "I think we ought at least to consider the possibility . . ." Is Catharine's story true? Was her performance real? We'll never know.

Early drafts of *Suddenly Last Summer* reveal how unsure Williams himself was of his ending, and the significance of the open ending he ultimately chose. The drafts include at least nine different versions of the doctor's closing speech, all of which are longer and more explanatory than the final version. One thing they disclose is the role of *Suddenly Last Summer* in Williams's interrogation of dramatic realism, the playwright's attempts to locate his own mode between what he terms "factual" and "visionary" truth: as the doctor puts it in one version, "There's two kinds of truth, at least. One is factual: the other is visionary: there's a lot of both in her story. I think it's the visionary part of it, I mean the end of the story, that meant more *to me more* than I could believe in. At least, anyhow—I'm not going to try to cut it out of her head . . ." This is a good description of Williams's dramaturgy, in which the visionary—fantasy, poetry, myth, and theater—is opposed to verisimilitude as such. Installing a wedge between these two kinds of truth, Williams defines his realism (such as it may be): the standard view of realist vision (as the light and enlightenment of knowledge) is transformed into Williams's "visionary" truth, far from "factual" reality. This visionary truth is, in another version of the ending, linked directly to the mind of madness:

> It always still shocks me a little to catch a glimpse of the world that violent patients strapped to cots at Lion's View have to witness and live in all the time. They take no walk in a garden, they live in no garden district, but in a strange way there are times when their perception seems to be clearer than ours!—that's when I'm shocked, and I don't *know* what to say . . .[32]

What is shocking to the doctor is the apprehension of the visionary perception of the insane, when all he sees are "violent patients strapped to cots." This vision of the psychiatric patients, what in the next lines he calls Catharine's "horribly vivid description of an image," halts the doctor's analytical description: "I don't know what to say . . ." As a commentary on drama and theater, the speech demonstrates Williams's ambivalence toward the psycho-logical (and speaks to the importance of locating him within a lineage of modernist melodrama): the spectacular, mad visions of theater take over rational, sane speech, and perhaps escape the playwright's authorial control. For if the doctor (as well as the playwright) doesn't know what to say, he also can't shut up: his verbosity in these early drafts suggests nothing so much as Catharine's own "babbling." In a countertransference of the patient's excessive monologues, now it is the doctor whose emotional memory resists narrative containment.

Just as Williams ends up departing from the logic of Aristotelean tragedy, rejecting an economy of truth and recognition for a system of repetition and recurrence, he abandons the comforts of explanation to make sense of chaos; in the end, he decided it was better to leave the honesty of its protagonist, and the honesty of his theater, in doubt than to close off the circuit of excitement that turns us all into Sebastians, tantalized by scenes of destruction, even (especially?) our own. *Suddenly Last Summer*, aligning the techniques of Method acting and the methods of psychoanalysis, shows how both further and multiply what they try to regulate and restrain: a mimetic desire—which is also a desire for mimesis—that always exceeds its bounds. Indeed, the ever-present possibility that Method acting's boundary-blurrings would lead to transgressive sexual desire was not lost on Lee Strasberg, who culled the title of his memoir from Hamlet's famous monologue: "Is it not monstrous that this player here / But in a fiction, in a dream of passion, / Could force his soul so to his own conceit . . . ?" In the tape-recorded Studio sessions, Strasberg comments on the monologue, mirroring Hamlet's incredulity:

Isn't it monstrous that someone should have this capacity? The profession of acting, the basic art of acting, is a monstrous thing because it is done with the same flesh-and-blood muscles with which you perform ordinary deeds, real deeds. The body with which you make real love is the same body with which you make fictitious love with someone whom you don't like, whom you fight with, whom you hate, by whom you hate to be touched. And yet you throw yourself into his arms with the same kind of aliveness and zest and passion as with your real lover—not only with your real lover, with your realest lover. In no other art do you have this monstrous thing.[33]

Strasberg's remarks demonstrate his awareness of the subversive sexual implications of the proximity between acting and being. Acting allows the monstrous confusion of unnatural object for natural one; more, it requires it. If Method acting was designed to maximize this intimacy between the "natural" sexual act and the "unnatural" one, it is perhaps the most monstrous kind of acting of all.

# Part Two

✦

*Political Methods*

# State Servant

...the Method that has done its service to the state and knows
it...
—Gordon Rogoff, "Lee Strasberg: Burning Ice," 1964

No indictment of Strasberg is more fascinating than Gordon Rogoff's
"Lee Strasberg: Burning Ice," published in 1964 in the *Tulane Drama
Review*. Rogoff had been the administrative director of the Actors Studio
from 1959 to 1960, during which time he was also an advisory editor at
the *Tulane Drama Review (TDR)* under Robert W. Corrigan; by 1964,
Richard Schechner had become editor of *TDR*, and Rogoff had left the
Studio. Parts of his essay, sprinkled with tart, barbed descriptions, read
like a Muriel Spark novel (Cheryl Crawford is described as having "lips
drawn tightly, nose set in sniffing readiness for the unacceptable odors
accompanying bad news, her entire frame poised, as it were, for that
Medea moment when she can dust the blackboard"); elsewhere it sounds
like an earnest, inflamed political pamphlet. For Rogoff's exposé, excori-
ating Strasberg's corruption, narcissism, manipulation, and stupidity ("in
Strasberg, the obvious presence of thought does little to hide the absence
of thinking"), is also a call to arms. The stagnant Actors Studio had produced almost nothing in its fifteen-plus years of operation, and certainly
nothing of worth, and it was time to unmask its deficiencies, some of the
most serious of which were political: its unblushing nationalism ("no one
else has ever built so systematically on the dogma of inherent American
superiority"), its ignorance of Brecht, and, most of all, its status as "diver-
sionary tactic," distracting American artists from the important work at
hand. This distraction is the "service to the state" that Rogoff refers to in
his breathless, run-on conclusion:

> While [actors] can be forgiven for hanging back with their dreams,
> for falling into the trap of certainty, for giving their lives to the only
> man who seemed to be there—through force of his own tenacity,
> his capacity for staying firmly rooted in the same earth for over
> thirty years—it is possible now that the arguments for and against
> this settled issue, this diversionary tactic—the Method that has done

its service to the state and knows it—that these arguments, and the
great battle for an American theatre, will have to be taken elsewhere,
leaving some of them behind; using what has been learned; discard-
ing what has clotted the brain and paralyzed action, movement, and
growth; building theatres where the eternal child will find no comfort,
where dramatists are respected, directors are encouraged, and where
actors no longer sing in chorus that their hearts belong to Daddy.[1]

The Method, here, is more than just a technique, and Strasberg more than
just a teacher. This is "the great battle for an American theater," against
a state-aligned, morally corrupt establishment that has "clotted the brain
and paralyzed action."

The rhetoric of Rogoff's conclusion is worth considering in light of the
political context it cannot help but evoke for a contemporary reader—the
Cold War—which is, indeed, the historical context in which Strasberg and
Method acting have most often been placed in contemporary scholarship.[2]
Generally, scholars have followed Rogoff (whether or not they follow his
negative judgment) in placing Strasberg on the side of American nationalism: Louis Scheeder, for instance, in his analysis of Strasberg's Method,
declares that "against the background of the Cold War and the depreda-
tions of the McCarthy era, Lee Strasberg transformed Russian theatrical
practice into a symbol of American freedom and nationalism."[3] But the
politics of Method acting during the Cold War are more complicated than
this account would suggest. First of all, understanding them necessitates
a close examination of Elia Kazan's 1952 testimony as a friendly witness before the House Un-American Activities Committee (HUAC), the
elephant in the background of Rogoff's condemnation: Kazan, after all,
was the literal state servant. His testimony at HUAC did indeed actively
align his kind of theater with American anticommunism: one play he'd
directed is "thoroughly and wonderfully American in its tone, characters, and outlook"; another is "deeply democratic and deeply optimistic."
Even the plays that were "not political" could be construed as patriotic:
one shows the "human courage and endurance in many kinds of people";
two others are "not political, but very human."[4] It is perhaps for this
reason that despite the Russian roots of Method acting, the committee's
line of questioning regarding Stanislavsky's influence on the American
theater did not go very far, although it did come up. Both Kazan and
Lee Cobb (another former Group Theatre member) portrayed the relationship between left-wing politics and their theatrical practice as one of
attempted, and rebuffed, infiltration. According to Kazan, it was because
the Communist Party wanted him to influence the actors' committee of

the Group Theatre and insisted that he apologize for not doing so that he became disillusioned with communism and left the party.[5]

Kazan's testimony is difficult to misread: he was an enthusiastic "friendly witness." But we might remark that the director's ritualistic repetition of the words "American," "democratic," and "human" evinces, in its very excessiveness, the force of compensation. Joseph Litvak argues that HUAC was never really about communist ideology but rather about purging the Jewish mimetic comedian, reading the persecution of Hollywood liberals—if not actually Jewish, then metonymically so—as the persecution of a particularly threatening kind of mimetic nonidentity that displays itself in the making of jokes, what he calls "comicosmopolitanism." By naming names, Kazan became, in Litvak's terms (adapted from Alain Badiou), a sycophant, a soldier in HUAC's war on comicosmopolitanism in which comic promiscuity must be destroyed in favor of normative and "deadly serious" American citizenship.[6] But Litvak argues that Kazan (and his sometime artistic collaborator, Budd Schulberg) was infected by the comic mimesis he tried to destroy: "Virtuosos of imitative betrayal, mimics of the mimesis they destroy, they pay, that is, the backhanded compliment of the flattery that attacks and the attack that flatters."[7] The victory over Jewish mimesis is never complete for the sycophant, who is always near the heels of the comicosmopolitan Jewish comedian, just as Kazan's "honesty" in front of the committee is clearly an imitation of what he imagines they want to hear:

> [Kazan] continued, even into old age, to epitomize the "Method," not least as a method for obeying the "other-directed' imperative to entertain by appearing to refuse it in favor of something far superior: the manly-yet-sensitive pursuit of Honesty . . . The humorlessness that is one of the clichés of Method acting—as that of that other Cold War phenomenon whose "Russian" accent is more pronounced, namely, Communism—reflects the skill with which Kazan himself, on-screen and off, practiced the seductive theatricality of antitheatricality, the *sprezzatura* of the twentieth-century courtier.[8]

Litvak suggests that the Method is the very emblem of Kazan's anxious sycophancy that slips into mimetic theatricality. The imperative to entertain infects Method acting's seriousness with a Jewish mimetic laughter, just as the Yiddish theater, where both Strasberg and his rival, Stella Adler, were reared, haunts Method acting—lest we forget the image of the Strasbergs as Svengalis, who manipulated and corrupted Marilyn Monroe with their sick, neurotic Method.[9]

This is part of what we miss in the simplistic conflation of Method acting with Kazan's patriotic anticommunism. After all, in the early 1960s,
Kazan purged himself of Strasberg as well, leaving the Actors Studio
for the Lincoln Center Repertory and largely breaking off their connection. Kazan's papers reveal the similarity between this purgation and his
decades-earlier rejection of communism: as he described his break from
the Party, after he refused to make the actors' committee of the Group
Theatre "a Communist mouthpiece," he revolted after being "invited
to go through a typical Communist scene of crawling and apologizing
and admitting the error of my ways."[10] In a note he wrote to himself
after leaving the Studio, he repeats a similar revulsion to his groveling in
front of Strasberg: "STOP APOLOGIZING. Strasberg is the last person
to whom you apologize, constantly . . . You got free of him once, now
for the last time, get away from this marginal tiny foolish remnant of
your father-terror . . . And his blaming you for his not doing more with
the Actors' [sic] Studio is sick. Just plain sick."[11] Strasberg becomes both
sick manipulator and "father-terror," echoing a familiar characterization of the Janus-faced communist. Something, too, of this accusation is
echoed in Rogoff's indictment of Strasberg, in which, despite its avowed
unmasking of the Method's right-wing authoritarianism, the acting guru's
evasions, dogmas, and mind games sound surprisingly similar to those of
"Red double-talk."[12]

To return to the contemporary political performance with which I
began this book, Obama's White House Correspondents' Dinner parody video: perhaps this political ambivalence inside the figuration of the
Method—both patriotic and hypocritical, both stand-up American and
neurotic Jew—is why, in 2013, Method acting was what our exceedingly
cosmopolitan president used to make a joke of his enemies' incredulity.
Raising the taboo of blackface alongside the still potent sense that Obama
is not *really* American, the video uses Method acting both to mock the
right-wing fantasy of national whiteness which renders Obama an infil-
trator with the mask of sincerity, like the Jewish actors whose Jewish
birth names HUAC "outed" as evidence of their foreign sympathies, and
to expose the actual regime of performance that fixes identity in the visual
field and denies mimetic mobility. Method acting, in Obama's video, is no
longer sycophantic, but dangerously comicosmopolitan; making fun of
Method acting by acting like you're Method acting—which means acting
like "yourself"—through vertiginous multiplications of mimesis is exactly
the "en-Jewment" that Litvak describes (suggesting, as well, that today
the comicosmopolitan has been transferred from the Jew to the immigrant and the terrorist).[13] The video tries to have it both ways: Obama's

comicosmopolitanism is dampened somewhat by the appearance of Tracy Morgan, who is not, after all, Joe Biden (how different would it have been if Joe Biden had appeared to declare he was Tracy Morgan?). The black body remains immutable. Or is that the joke? What about the choice of Morgan himself, whose own performances so often parody that very assumption of black immutability (his most famous character, an actor/comedian named Tracy Jordan on the TV show *30 Rock*, is a parody of the racist stereotype of an uneducated, materialistic black celebrity)? When Robert Gibbs told reporters that Obama believed in action rather than Method acting, he was controlling the fear of Obama's mimesis; now Obama appears to flaunt it, answering the omnipresent inquiry of his presidential tenure, "What *is* he?" with the threatening reply of the cosmopolitan: "I could be *anything*."

Obama's video gives me a key point of entry for the following two chapters, as it lays bare the challenge racial difference proffers to Method acting's universalism, an insight I trace to James Baldwin. Obama's video teasingly inquires whether the performance of Americanness, represented by the protean Method actor, will be able to assimilate Obama; James Baldwin, in the early 1960s, had a similar question, although for him it had very different stakes. What theatrical methods would be able to represent African American life, in both realistic and politically motivating ways? Obama's video uses Method acting as a figure for his apparent ability to transcend his own difference (and something of a dare to those who would deny it), but Baldwin was looking for a different solution, one that would not merely assimilate the black actor and black character to structures of national whiteness. Baldwin came to believe that the Method's model of identification and the universalism that went along with it led to an erasure of difference and of history that produced the same effect as the political imposition of a unified American identity: the invisibility of marginalized people and the silencing of dissent. In my analysis of Baldwin's *Blues for Mister Charlie* and the New York production of Jean Genet's *The Blacks* (originally *Les Nègres*), I uncover a vector of pressure on Method acting that has been little studied: the increasing sense that both Method acting and the realist drama aligned with it were incapable of representing African American experience.

Chapter 3

✦

# The Method and the Means: James Baldwin at the Actors Studio

In the climactic scene of James Baldwin's 1968 novel, *Tell Me How Long the Train's Been Gone*, the narrator and protagonist, Leo Proudhammer, appears with his friend and lover Barbara in the living room of a Jewish acting teacher named Saul San-Marquand, artistic director of the Actors' Means Workshop. Leo and Barbara have been hanging around the small town in New Jersey where the Workshop has gone for the summer season, and finally have been given their promised chance to perform a scene for Saul, who will decide on the basis of that scene whether or not they'll be accepted as members of the Workshop. They have prepared a scene from Clifford Odets's *Waiting for Lefty*, in which the young couple, Flor and Sid, break off their relationship under pressure from Flor's brother. Leo, who is black, and Barbara, who is white, have just admitted their love for one another: their impossible interracial relationship underlies Baldwin's novel. When they arrive in Saul's living room, they have just walked through town together to the obscene and threatening jeers of the white townspeople, validating their decision, made in bed hours earlier, that their relationship can never be public.

As they enter Saul's living room, they come upon a young actor performing a monologue from *Othello*. Leo is the only black person associated with the Workshop; Baldwin describes the other actor as "swarthy." His performance is a parody of bad acting: overwrought but emotionally nonsensical; physical but without life; superficial and thoughtless. It is obvious to Leo that this is bad acting, but Saul and the other students don't seem to think so. When the actor is asked to explain himself, he says that he was trying to make Othello's emotions physical: "Grief, for me, always goes to my stomach." Saul's response is cautiously positive: "We feel . . . that you have made very nice progress since you have been with us . . . You are less afraid than you were of letting us see your insides, so to say." The actor's flailing is passed off as personal revelation.[1] When the discussion turns to the question of Othello's race, the acting student denies—glancing guiltily at Leo—that his race makes a difference. Saul congratulates him on his work: "We admire the direct-ness of your approach to your problem—the idea of Othello with, so to say, a bellyache, we do not reject, as others might, no, we find it a very interesting idea."[2]

When Barbara and Leo play their scene, Saul is nowhere near as gentle. He is snide, imperious, and caustically vague. He criticizes their choice of scene, expressing his doubt that they could have any sense of the play. Saul tells Leo that he finds his "equipment for the theater extremely meager." The problem is his body: "An actor's instrument is his body, is himself. Paul Robeson, for example, is an actor who was made to play Othello. The instrument suggests it, the instrument, so to say, demands it. Other actors could never play Othello. The instrument could not carry the illu-sion." Saul is implying, none too subtly, that Leo's race is the intractable limit of his acting ability. He will never get around it, and therefore he will never be a competent actor in the white world. "You were bom-bastic, hysterical, and self-pitying"—not only did Leo's black body not go with the part, but there was something excessive about that body in performance, "bombastic, hysterical." Unlike Leo's disdainful summa-tion of the swarthy young actor's Othello, which was so disconnected from the character's emotion that passionate grief turned into a stom-achache, Saul's criticism of Leo is that his emotionality was too much, over-the-top, sentimental—unfitting and unbecoming. The only part of Leo's performance that Saul approves of is his soft-shoe routine at the end of the scene: "Then you seemed free, and, so to say, joyous and boy-ish . . . If we decide to continue with you . . . it will be in the hope that we can make such moments come more easily to you."[3] In other words, Leo should stick to minstrelsy.


## Baldwin and the Studio

Saul San-Marquand, of course, is Lee Strasberg; the "Means" is the Method; this is what Baldwin, in 1968, had to say about the Actors Studio. The sat-ire is so bellicose and so thinly veiled that one might wonder at Baldwin's bitterness. Ten years earlier he had felt quite differently. Baldwin had a long and productive association with the Actors Studio, beginning in 1958, when the Studio tried out a dramatic version of Baldwin's novel *Giovanni's Room*. Shortly after the workshop, Baldwin returned from a trip to Paris to assist Kazan on his direction of two productions: Archibald MacLeish's *JB* and Tennessee Williams's *Sweet Bird of Youth*.[4] Kazan hoped that Baldwin would become a full-fledged Studio playwright, and Baldwin participated in the Playwrights Unit that Kazan set up at the Studio for the season of 1959–60, alongside Norman Mailer and Edward Albee.[5] According to both Baldwin and Kazan, it was Kazan's suggestion that Baldwin write a play about the murder of Emmett Till, which eventually became *Blues for Mister Charlie*, Baldwin's best-known play, which premiered in an Actors Studio production on Broadway in 1964.[6]

That play and that production are the subject of this chapter. *Blues for Mister Charlie* sits at the hinge of Baldwin's politics, between the liberal Baldwin of the 1950s and the more radical Baldwin of the 1960s and 1970s, and *Tell Me How Long the Train's Been Gone*, Baldwin's only work of fiction to directly deal with the politics of that time, demonstrates the intimate connection between this political transition and Baldwin's experience with the Actors Studio. Both the novel and the play reveal how Baldwin's critique of Method acting and its model of psychological identification catalyzed his growing discontentment with liberal universalism. Both works also illustrate Baldwin's struggle to articulate a third way between the universalism that Method acting modeled—and that had characterized Baldwin's own voice as a young writer—and the separatism he would later embrace. In *Tell Me How Long the Train's Been Gone*, this struggle yielded a novel that critics found baggy, moralistic, and sentimental.[7] In *Blues for Mister Charlie*, this struggle generated a problematic, even schizophrenic, dramatic structure and tone. But it also sparked a searching reflection on the difficulties intrinsic to the performance of racial difference in a theatrical culture that insists on a particular kind of identification. Increasingly discontent with the Method and American realist theater, but not willing to leave behind his belief in the power of empathic identification and the individual consciousness, Baldwin wrote a play that engaged the politics of his historical moment through a complex interrogation of theatrical form. The play reveals not only a crucial contour of its author's artistic and political trajectory, but also how deeply Method acting was intertwined with the political concerns of its time.

The Actors Studio production of *Blues for Mister Charlie* was, by all accounts, a turbulent experience for those involved. Strasberg became the artistic director of the Studio in 1951, and by 1960, Kazan had left and was working on a new production company at Lincoln Center; he wanted Baldwin to do *Blues for Mister Charlie* there, but Baldwin decided to give it to the new directors of the Actors Studio instead. Whatever Baldwin's motives for doing so—his biographer James Campbell suggests he was playing out an Oedipal conflict with Kazan; Robert Cordier opined at the time that Baldwin "wanted the Actors Studio badge"—it was an ill-starred match from the first.[8] The rehearsal process was plagued with endless conflict: the Studio directors thought the play was too long (the original script ran at five hours), too confusing (the action moves back and forth in time without clear delineation), too offensive (Studio producer Cheryl Crawford was particularly upset about all the curse words), and, most of all, too polemical. Baldwin fought back at every point—he refused (against protocol for a playwright) to relinquish control, and insisted that Frank Corsaro be fired as director and that Burgess Meredith replace him—and everyone disliked each other by the end. Baldwin was discontented enough with his experience to remark that he wouldn't give the Actors Studio another play of his "unless I'm attacked with leprosy of the brain."[9] This dramatic shift in Baldwin's view of the Studio was matched by a political shift that, by 1964, had reached a pitch: increasingly sensitive to the criticisms of black writers like Amiri Baraka, who had accused him of pandering to the white elite, he dedicated his play to Medgar Evers and "the dead children of Birmingham" and told *Playbill* that he had written the play "on pads in planes, trains, gas stations" in the South while traveling for the civil rights movement; whether or not this is true, it speaks to Baldwin's concern that the play be taken as an authentic statement of an artist *engagé*.[10]

Baldwin had never been shy about declaring that mainstream American theater was depressingly safe and apolitical. He disliked Edward Albee's "race problem" play, *The Death of Bessie Smith*, and concluded that the central problem of the American theater was its ineptitude at handling the real lives of blacks. This he made explicit in his 1961 article "Theater: The Negro In and Out": "Much of the American confusion, if not most of it, is a direct result of the American effort to avoid dealing with the Negro as a man. The theater cannot fail to reflect this confusion, with results which are unhealthy for the white actor, and disastrous for the Negro." The primary target of this article is incompetent playwriting: "In search of a truth which is not in the script, [actors] are reduced to what seem to be psychotherapeutic exercises. Listening to actors talk about the means they employ to 'justify' this line, or that action, is enough to break the heart and set the teeth on edge."[11] These "psychotherapeutic exercises" and searches for justifications are direct references to Method acting. In 1961, at least, Baldwin directed his criticism at American realist drama; realist acting, Method acting, he presents as a somewhat pathetic attempt to create truth where there is none: false writing "cannot fail, finally, to have a terrible effect on the actor's art."[12] After the complicated experience of *Blues for Mister Charlie*, however, he came to different conclusions about the source of American theater's problems.

*Blues for Mister Charlie* was Baldwin's attempt to write a counterhegemonic realist drama. Its first two acts use realist idiom to dramatize the ideological conflict that was taking shape in the public consciousness, between integration, passive resistance, and conciliation on the one hand, and separatism and militant revolt on the other. What happens to that realism by the third act, however, reveals Baldwin's increasing skepticism that its terms could achieve his political goals. In *Blues*, Baldwin associates realism with liberal humanism, represented by upstanding black citizen Reverend Meridian Henry, dedicated to the Christian ethic of turning the other cheek. When his son Richard is murdered by a white man, Lyle Britten, Reverend Meridian begins to question the wisdom of his philosophy. In the third act, which takes place entirely in the courtroom, Baldwin abandons realist convention entirely: the two crowds on the two sides of the courtroom, representing "Whitetown" and "Blacktown," speak in chorus, commenting on the action as if they were in a Brecht play. The characters, as well, speak directly to the audience, and the action flashes forward and backward in time. Following Britten's acquittal for the murder, Reverend Meridian decides to follow the black students of the town and pick up the gun. The play's abandonment of realism signals its abandonment of Meridian's conciliatory humanism.

It is not surprising that *Blues for Mister Charlie* "marks the end of [Baldwin's] season as white liberal America's black darling."[13] But even the third act of *Blues* spends substantial time more or less sympathetically exploring the psyche of the white liberal character, Parnell James, and the play's final lines find Juanita, a radicalized black student, inviting him, if grudgingly, to march alongside her. Baldwin was ambivalent about his play's conclusions, just as he was clearly ambivalent about his decision to give the play to the nearly all-white Actors Studio to be produced on white Broadway.[14] Who was this play for? Even the title is ambiguous: is the play *for* Mister Charlie (is Mister Charlie the white Broadway audience)? If so, how does that complicate the representation of race in the play, if it is, in some sense, a performance of blackness for whites? Could the title be ironic? Or is the play about the blues *of* Mister Charlie, a mourning song for Mister Charlie's moral and emotional failings? Then there is Baldwin's odd turn of phrase in a remark to journalists that he wanted his audience "to be sitting on the edge of your chair waiting for the nurses to carry you out."[15] That description's tension between the active and the passive—you're sitting at attention, ostensibly ready to act, but instead, nurses carry your passive body out—reflects Baldwin's equivocation.

Baldwin wrote his play for a certain kind of actor, the kind of actor he helped Kazan direct in 1958 and knew would be cast in an Actors Studio production: a Method actor. But, as I will argue, Baldwin's play was also written *against* the Method actor, challenging Method acting's psychological hermeneutic and the kind of universalism it puts forth. It also plays out the conflict between the exigencies of playwriting and those of performance that had been an issue since Boleslavsky.[16] Baldwin preempted this power struggle by writing a play that included pedagogic instructions on how to play his characters. Teaching actors how to read and interpret his intentions, he offered them (or some of them) an alternative mode of performance, one that could better articulate his artistic and political goals.

## The Psychological Hermeneutic

In part 1, I outlined the psychological debates around hysteria and hypnosis in a mostly European context. But psychology in the United States has its own complex history, of which its views on and treatment of race are a central part. The 1910s saw the development of what was called race psychology. Catalyzed by the so-called Negro education debate, an offshoot of the segregation debate, race psychology evolved out of eugenic theory, studying psychological differences between races, and its conclusions overwhelmingly supported racist stereotypes: Negroes were unintelligent, lazy, overemotional, and so on. By the 1930s, liberal psychologists had begun to denounce race psychology as racist in its assumptions and conclusions; in fact, Graham Richards argues that it was psychology's criticism of race psychology that led to the recognition of racism itself as a psychological category and a social fact.[17] The idea that racism and prejudice should be the objects of psychological study instead of racial difference itself came out of the social psychology and culture and personality schools, both explicitly antiracist. But as Richards points out, even these schools had the racist foundational assumption that white culture was the norm from which other cultures deviated.[18] This was also the assumption of military psychologists during World War II, when black soldiers' problematic identification with the United States became a matter of concern.

At the same time, American psychologists were developing the notion of a national character and personality. Psychological anthropologists like Margaret Mead and Ruth Benedict wrote about the psychological profile of national cultures; Benedict even defined culture as "personality writ large."[19] After the war, these views carried forward, just as the increasingly important role of psychoanalysts, psychiatrists, and psychologists in the war effort carried forward into postwar policy and ideology. During this era psychoanalytic concepts became widely popularized, "part of the psychological common sense" of American culture.[20] Policy makers as well as researchers of all kinds embraced psychology as the answer to social as well as individual problems. This broadly impacted the discourse surrounding race and the way the United States government responded to the first waves of political protests that became the civil rights movement, which government-sponsored psychologists diagnosed as case studies in "community disorders." However, by the mid-1960s, there was a backlash against what was called the "damaged Negro" model: the model of a catastrophically damaged black psyche in need of psychological (as opposed to political or economic) help. The Moynihan Report of 1965, "The Negro Family: The Case for National Action," provoked a wave of criticism for turning the myriad problems faced by black Americans into problems of ego, self-image, and gender identity. As Ellen Herman puts it, tellingly, "After decades of performing as walking, talking examples of racism's psychological destruction, black Americans had had enough."[21] As Herman's turn of phrase suggests, part of what was so problematic about postwar psychological theories of race was the way they imposed all-encompassing hermeneutics of performance.

In his introduction to the play, which he wrote immediately before its premiere, Baldwin makes his challenge to the "damaged Negro" model clear. The introduction begins by describing how he "absolutely dreaded" writing it because of his "fear that [he] would never be able to draw a valid portrait of the murderer." He then describes addressing this problem of characterization, the problem of the "valid portrait," with two rather surprising tactics. First, he insists that "we, the American people" take responsibility for creating this monster: "We have created him, he is our servant." Second, he offers what seems like a Freudian reading of historical crime as individual trauma:

> What is ghastly and really almost hopeless in our racial situation now is that the crimes we have committed are so great and unspeakable that the acceptance of this knowledge would lead, literally, to madness. The human being, then, in order to protect himself, closes his eyes, compulsively repeats his crimes, and enters a spiritual darkness which no one can describe.[22]

The "unspeakable" crime is repressed; as in Freud's model of trauma, the inability to process the past event leads to a compulsive repetition of it. What are we to make, though, of Baldwin's insistence that these crimes are all of ours—including, he strongly implies, those of us who are black? This acceptance of collective responsibility is less shocking if we consider it in the context of contemporaneous psychological discourse. Baldwin's introduction turns the "damaged Negro" model around: the racist is Frankenstein's monster here, created by a corrupt culture, stumbling blindly through the repetition of his crimes. His play enacts the same reversal: in *Blues for Mister Charlie*, it is white psychology that is damaged. Black responsibility, furthermore, is also black agency: taking on the ethical responsibility of grasping the psychology of the white racist, Baldwin highlights his own intellectual and artistic action, just as his play highlights the decisive political action of his black characters. The play, as I will show, contrasts the trauma-filled and guilt-ridden behavior of the "damaged whites" with the increasingly collective action of the black characters; however, it ultimately presents psychological analysis and radical action as competing strategies and, to some extent, mutually exclusive ones.

However, as I have suggested, the play is more ambivalent about this trade-off than its conclusion suggests. The outlier in the play's dramaturgy is Richard Henry, who, swaggering and slang-speaking, refuses to play the Jim Crow game: he carries a gun, brags about sleeping with white women in New York, scoffs at the cowering ways of the town's black population, and doesn't hide his disdain for Lyle or dodge his threats. For these reasons, Richard has confused and repelled critics since the play's premiere: they have tended to see him as "a stereotypical provocateur, a cardboard cut-out whose final telos is nothing more than a meaningless, avoidable death at the hands of a white bigot."[23] This view of Richard as a "cardboard cut-out" strikes me as a baffling misreading. The most fully drawn and psychologically complex character in the play, Richard is also the artist (a singer, "much loved on the Apollo Theatre stage in Harlem," who returns from New York to his family in the South), and thus to some extent Baldwin's proxy.[24] As Meredith Malburne argues, Lyle and Richard are characters "Baldwin wished to make human rather than uncomplicated types . . . more than simply radical representations of white and black."[25] Baldwin's introduction focuses on his own challenges with his characterization of Lyle Britten; Richard, however, is a challenge to the Method's model of psychological characterization as such. Can a white audience (both the predominantly white audience of Broadway, and the mostly white membership of the Studio) look at a black man on the stage and see what Method acting (perhaps naively, perhaps disingenuously) insisted it should see: an individual with a unique history but nonetheless recognizable and identifiable emotions and motivations?

And what about the symbol Richard becomes, the symbol that catalyzes the black characters' resistance to racist violence and injustice? The final scene in the courtroom, which does emphatically reject psychological explanation in favor of political action, has been read as the failure of Baldwin the writer in the face of Baldwin the activist, but this reading ignores the fact that Baldwin undercuts his black characters' polemics. After all, whether they know it or not—Baldwin leaves this ambiguous—their characterizations of Richard are untrue: Richard *did* have a gun; he *did* brag about pictures of himself with white women. This underscores Baldwin's ambivalence toward Richard's martyrdom. After all, Richard is the most individualistic character in *Blues*, the one who most struggles with group identification; only in death could Richard be a symbol for community coherence. Is Richard more important as an individual or as a symbol? The play keeps knocking against the question, not content to have it either way. Baldwin does not just critique the white self-justifications for racial oppression; he also, more subtly, questions the militant black response. The movement needs a heroic image, not an imperfect, psychologically complicated person. But what is lost in that transmutation?

## The Politics of Theatrical Form

*Blues for Mister Charlie* opens with Richard's murder, without context, and without individuation: "In the darkness we hear a shot." The lights go up on Lyle, standing over Richard's body: "And may every nigger end like this nigger—face down in the weeds!" This symbolic genocide is immediately subverted in the play's first scene between Reverend Meridian and the black students Tom, Ken, and Arthur:

> MERIDIAN: No, no, no! You have to say it like you mean it—the way they really say it: nigger, nigger, nigger! *Nigger!* Tom, the way *you* saying it, it sounds like you just *might* want to be friends. And that's not the way they sound out there. Remember all that's happened. Remember we having a funeral here—tomorrow night. Remember why. Go on, hit it again.
>
> TOM: You dirty nigger, you no-good black bastard, what you doing down here, anyway?
>
> MERIDIAN: That's much better. Much, much better. Go on.[26]

Ostensibly, Meridian is instructing the students in passive resistance, showing them what they will have to withstand when they protest Richard's death. But what is so striking about this opening scene is how much it is about acting the parts of the racists. Meridian is coaching them on

good acting: "Say it like you mean it," say it "the way they really say it"—
say it, also, the way we've just heard the actor playing Lyle Britten say it,
in the play's opening line. Baldwin presents this acting class as a necessary
psychological prerequisite to political action. Even more interestingly, the
way he coaches them to say it "the way they really say it" is by referenc-
ing not what they may have remembered hearing, but the present trauma,
which does not have a direct correlation to their performance. Instead, he
suggests a kind of emotional metonymy, or substitution; in other words,
a kind of emotional memory: "Remember we having a funeral here—
tomorrow night. Remember why." The way to coax a good performance
out of them is not to have them imitate someone else's feeling but to get
them in touch with their own: "Remember all that's happened." Good
acting here requires finding a correspondence between your own experience and the character's. Meridian is teaching them Method acting.

Cindy Patton has argued that Method acting enabled the move away
from overtly racist, stereotypical performances of blacks in American
popular culture: according to her, Method acting made the performances
of black actors seem real, and their suffering seem authentic, enabling
mainstream white audiences to identify with their plight. We should not
underestimate how much Method acting in cinema did, she maintains,
to change racial mores, and how intertwined the transformation of cinematic representation of African Americans, via Method acting, was with
the political goals of the civil rights movement. Authentic performance
of black characters by black actors was considered by many as itself a
political goal: "The power of authentic presence was understood to be
capable of decentering inauthentic and inauthentically held prejudice.
This was a basic premise of the civil rights movement and, I suggest,
of all identity-based social movements that followed."[27] Although Patton
restricts her analysis to film, suggesting that the film genre most suited to
Method acting was melodrama (especially "race problem" melodrama),
her argument for the usefulness of Method acting as a way to dispel racial
stereotypes in acting in the midcentury resonates with *Blues*—at least it
resonates with the point of view represented by Reverend Meridian in
this opening scene. Baldwin ultimately came to different conclusions.

Almost immediately, the play interrupts its portrayal of the realist
performance of character, as the Method acting, directed by Meridian,
suddenly turns real:

> MERIDIAN: Why you all standing around there like that? Go on and
> get you a nigger. Go on!

(*A scuffle.*)

MERIDIAN: All right. All right! Come on, now. Come on.

(*Ken steps forward and spits in Arthur's face.*)

ARTHUR: You black s.o.b., what the hell do you think you're doing?
    You mother—!

MERIDIAN: Hey, hold it! Hold it! Hold it!

(*Meridian wipes the boy's face. They are all trembling.*)[28]

Method acting wanted to create real life on stage. But how real is too real? Ken so completely identifies with his role as a racist that he spits in Arthur's face. But this physical violence, the effect of a truly successful performance of character, is so real that it destroys the logic of character acting itself: it breaks the scene. It also introduces the threat that hangs over the rest of the play—that theatrical violence could turn into real violence. Like the music, like the nonmimetic spaces of the church and courtroom, Ken's spit breaks the representational logic that underlies realist acting. It confuses the border between fact and fiction that Method acting was intended to complicate but, ultimately, to control.

*Blues* aligns Method acting with the liberal universalism and Christian empathy practiced by the Reverend Meridian: well meant, and ineffective. The play rejects both, on the level of content (Meridian decides, at the close of the play, to keep Richard's gun), and formally in the play's continued rupture of representational space, which, by the time we get to the third act in the presentational courtroom, has completely taken over. The opening stage directions specify that "each witness, when called, is revealed behind scrim and passes through two or three tableaux before moving down the aisle to the witness stand"—a far cry from the "fourth wall" directions at the top of the second act: "Jo and an older woman, Hazel, have just taken a cake out of the oven."[29] Baldwin pointedly places the witnesses in the same positions in relation to the audience as he did Meridian ("the witness stand is downstage, in the same place, and at the same angle as the pulpit in Acts I and II"), to the same effect: the witnesses are both in the scene and in the real space of the theater, actually addressing the real audience. Again, Baldwin highlights the presentational style of this performance with a song, heard before the curtain rises, to further emphasize that whatever is going on onstage is real, not virtual, action.

The formal differences between the tableaux that precede the characters' testimonies correspond to these different levels of theatricality. In Jo Britten's tableaux, introduced by a stage direction that places her "at a church social," her lines locate her inside her memory of the church event where Lyle first paid attention to her, then at their wedding. In these expressionistic scenes, she performs the memories that will influence her psychological state during her testimony, causing her to lie and say that Richard tried to rape her, in order to absolve her husband of his crime. Crucially, however, the tableaux given to the characters after Jo do not, like hers do, take us away from the event of the play; rather, they dramatize hidden parts of it: when Papa D., the black owner of a juke joint, takes the stand, we flash back to the moments in his juke joint before Richard's murder. Similarly, when Lorenzo, a black student and Richard's friend, is called, we flash to a scene of him and Pete in jail for protesting Richard's murder.

Juanita's flashback, which follows Lorenzo's, begins, like Jo's, in monologue, and includes a stage direction that places her in the scene, but unlike Jo's monologue, Juanita's speech does not place her in the same scene as the stage direction does: it situates her in real time describing a past event. As with the others, Juanita's testimony is also accompanied by a mimetic scene, but by contrast, this scene is intrinsic to Juanita's testimony:

THE STATE: You met whom?

JUANITA: I met—Richard.

(*We discover Meridian.*)

MERIDIAN: Hello Juanita. Don't look like that.[30]

Juanita's testimony transforms the convention of the tableaux/courtroom scenes. Previously the internal narration moved back and forth from past to present in order to represent the characters' individual psychic states. Jo Britten's memory of the church basement is not on the same level of dramatic action as her testimony: the false dialogue in which we hear her voice alone, and her confessional tone—she is obviously not really saying half the things she "says"—serve to emphasize that what we are seeing belongs to her character exclusively, her psychological past that explains her actions in the present. But in Juanita's tableaux and testimony, the present action and the past experience are fused, their boundaries blurred. Now the represented memory and the stage event are on the same level. Just as the musical interludes and Meridian's sermons fuse mimetic action with performative action, the temporal fusing of past and present in Juanita's testimony directs us not to a fictional play-world, but to the reality of the theatrical event at hand. We are out of psychology.

The rest of the play links this transformation of representative logic to the increased theatrical power of the black characters. When the state calls the Reverend Meridian to the stand, instead of a psychologically revealing vignette, we see him preaching at Sunday school. When the state lawyer's questioning becomes pointedly sexual, as he tries to push Meridian toward a pseudo-Freudian explanation of Richard's deviance in terms of Oedipal conflict and perversion, Meridian refuses to discuss psychology or psychological motive at all: "Your judgment of myself and my motives cannot concern me." Instead he uses the stand as a pulpit (further blurring the line between the flashback and the present scene) and polemicizes against "*your* guns, *your* hoses, *your* dogs, *your* judges, *your* law-makers, *your* folly, *your* pride, *your* cruelty, *your* cowardice, *your* money, *your* chain gangs, and *your* churches!"[31] When the final witness, Parnell, the white liberal who finds himself caught between loyalties, returns in his tableaux to a scene as psychologically explanatory as Jo Britten's—an episode of impotence with a white woman reminds him of his erotic obsession with blackness and adolescent romance with a black girl—the distinction becomes clear. The white characters are the ones stuck in their psychology, replaying the memories that explain their motives in the terms of psychosexual wounds and desires. When Lyle Britten is called to the stand, he is given two mimetic tableaux monologues, one in the woods and one in Papa D.'s juke joint, but no cross-examination at all: "*As Lyle approaches the witness stand, the lights in the courtroom dim.*"[32] No speech, no action, just explanatory memories: pushing Lyle out of the present stage action and back into character psychology, Baldwin leaves him in the weakest position of all.[33] The black characters, in contrast, are no longer determined by their psychology or required to abide by the representational realism of the "fourth wall." They literally take control of the theater.

By the end of *Blues for Mister Charlie*, Baldwin has aligned psychology with "Whitetown," while the black characters have traded it for political action. The decreased use of realist stage convention goes along with a decreased reliance on character psychology; both go along with the increased theatrical power of the black characters. Baldwin does not deny the psychological impact of racism and racist ideology, but his play does suggest that recognizing that trauma is no longer enough. How do we *break* the cycle of psychological repetition? How do we stop (Method) acting— and start really *acting*? Baldwin's experience working with the Studio could only have furthered his sense that the structures and tropes of psychological realism would not lead to the kind of theater his politics required.

### "Human Emotions"

When the Actors Studio took *Blues for Mister Charlie* to London to play at the World Theater Festival in 1965, it was an unambiguous disaster.

The production had been arranged at the last minute, and most of the star actors were missing, including Diana Sands as Juanita, and Rip Torn as Lyle Britten, which surely didn't help. But the London critics were almost uniformly vitriolic: one called it a "straggling, overloaded propaganda tract." There was a strong current of bald racism in the response: on opening night, members of the fascist British National Party heckled the actors, "Filth, why don't you go back to Africa?" But instead of confronting the British critics, Strasberg gave an infamous press conference in which he apologized for the play and its author: "There is a confusion between Mr. Baldwin's dynamic anger at the racial situation and the human involvement beneath it . . . It is partly his fault, partly ours, if the human emotions are not sufficiently conveyed in the production." Strasberg also explained that many of the actors in the London production were not regular Studio actors, and therefore the Studio should not be judged by their failings. His impolitic remarks shocked even those who knew him well. The notorious incident is likely what pushed Baldwin's opinion of Strasberg over the edge and led to the vituperative portrait in *Tell Me How Long the Train's Been Gone* with which I began this chapter.[34]

What is most revealing in Strasberg's remarks is his division of "dynamic anger" and "the human emotions beneath it": the distinction between emotion in the service of politics ("dynamic anger *at the racial situation*") and apolitical "human emotions." Particularity (and politics) are out, "universality" is in. Some emotional responses are "human," others are not. It is furthermore revealing that this facile racism accommodated what would seem to be the opposite view of Baldwin's play: that rather than including too few emotions, it deployed too many. In his review of *Blues*, Philip Roth memorably wrote, "If there ever is a Black Muslim nation, and if there is a television in that nation, then something like Acts Two and Three of *Blues for Mr. Charlie* will probably be the kind of thing the housewives will watch on afternoon TV."[35] Roth imagines a future nation in which the play's politics have become so hegemonic that they can be consumed as sentimental kitsch: like a soap opera, the play is too simplistic, too histrionic, too effeminate, too emotional.

Roth's comment is fascinatingly reactionary: how frightening the masculinist rhetoric of the Nation of Islam must have been to require a set of housewives to feminize it. Indeed, his use of the "sentimental" epithet, like Strasberg's division of human and nonhuman emotions, is a version of the exclusionary politics of emotion that the Workshop scene in *Tell Me How Long the Train's Been Gone* is meant to expose: "You were bombastic, hysterical and self-pitying," Saul San-Marquand/Strasberg told Leo/Baldwin. Opening with the white actor's insultingly simplistic identification with Othello, praised by San-Marquand, and finishing with San-Marquand's citation of Paul Robeson's *Othello* as evidence that black actors should only play black characters (and not attempt to understand the white class struggle), the climactic scene reveals the hidden perimeters of Method acting's universalism: white is universal, while black is always particular.

The third act of *Blues* is highly emotional, but clearly its entrance into what Eve Sedgwick called "the circumference of the sentimental" was intentional: Baldwin wanted the plight of the black characters to activate an emotional response in his largely white audience. This is a different kind of identification than the identification supported by psychological realism and represented in Jo and Lyle Britten's flashbacks. Juanita's monologue, inserted in the play immediately after she is called to testify, is the most striking example of this transformation. Urgently presentational, Juanita's monologue, in which she describes having sex with Richard, works to create an emotional effect outside individual psychology. It is, first of all, unprecedentedly *general*, full of abstract nouns without adjectives or qualifiers: "How he clung, how he struggled—life and death!" What could be a personal, intimate, even internal experience (of love and sexual intimacy) becomes the most elemental of struggles: "life and death." How much more universal can you get? "I want a lover made of flesh and blood, flesh and blood, like me!" she declares, later in her speech, again invoking elemental physicality against the one-sided particularizations of racism. But this all-inclusiveness is cut short when she unexpectedly breaks in with a direct address to the audience: "One more illegitimate black baby—that's right, you jive mothers!" This is a double interruption, with its interpolation of dialogue (the voice of the judgmental audience member) and its abrupt use of slang ("you jive mothers"). From an oceanic openness to a sudden particularization: this cutting intervention, addressed to the white audience, suspends and throws into relief their presumed sympathy with her supposedly universal experience of anguished love ("life and death," "flesh and blood"), pointing instead to the historically specific effects of her particular, raced experience ("one more illegitimate black baby").[36]

But although the monologue refuses the causal relations of psychology, it is not a clear-cut refusal of Method acting. In fact, in both form and content, it suggests a Strasbergian emotional memory exercise: Juanita begins by narrating a past sensory experience ("he lay beside me like a rock") before moving the memory into the emotional present, and throughout, she uses physical sensations to evoke emotion ("the smell, the

touch, the taste, the sound, of anguish!").[37] Even at its angriest, the monologue is not a call to arms; it is a powerful emotional memory that blurs
the line between past experience and present feeling, between the narration of a remembered event and the performance of a present emotion.
Juanita even ends with the exhausted conclusion "You're going crazy,
Juanita," incorporating the pervasive critical reaction to the Method
actress and her uncontrollable emotions, the same one sustained by Roslyn (in *The Misfits*) and Catharine (in *Suddenly Last Summer*): "she's
crazy."

Thus Baldwin wavers on Method acting's failure. Is the Method inherently racist, contributing to a model of American subjectivity from which
blacks are excluded? Or is there something like a black Method to be
found—a realist style that would renovate its terms from a black perspective? For despite his scorn for Saul San-Marquand and the Actors Means
Workshop, Leo Proudhammer, the protagonist of *Tell Me How Long the
Train's Been Gone*, is unquestionably a Method actor:

> I don't think I'd have minded if I could have found a role which had
> some relation to the life I lived, the life I knew, some role which did
> not traduce entirely my own sense of life, of my own life. But I played
> waiters, butlers, porters, clowns; since they had never existed in life,
> there was no conceivable way to play them. And one learned, there-
> fore, and long before one had learned anything else, the most abject
> reliance on the most shameful tricks, one learned before one learned
> anything else that contempt for the audience which is death to art.
> One was imitating an artifact, one might as well have been an icon,
> and one's performance depended not at all on what one saw—still
> less, God forbid, on what one felt—but on what the audience had
> come to see, had been trained to see.[38]

Like he did during the scene at the Actors Means' Workshop, Leo here
casts the problem of American theater as the problem of the performance
of race. The roles he is consigned to play are lifeless stereotypes, because
the audience does not want to understand the real lives of blacks: they
want their cozy racism affirmed. In opposition to this, Leo takes a position that is the Method's: the actor must be able to connect the role to
his life experience, must abhor "tricks" and instead really live on stage,
must, above all, not imitate, but actually feel. The sharp distinction Leo
Proudhammer makes between the imitation of racist stereotypes and the
truthful portrayal of "my own sense of life" is at the heart of Method
acting. Whatever his dismay at the racist undercurrents of Strasberg's

Studio, Baldwin did not completely dismiss Method acting's guiding theories. Perhaps this is why there is something disheartening in the otherwise galvanizing end of *Blues*: the sense that, in the necessary move toward political action, something might be lost. Richard's complexity, his contradictions, his youthful rebelliousness (which is only later, and then only partially, revolutionary), his artist's nonconformity—we mourn these, along with the institutional and cultural racism that allows white murderers to go free. Leo Proudhammer, perhaps speaking for his author, is constantly bewildered by the political role he feels it is his duty to take; *Blues* previews what in *Tell Me How Long the Train's Been Gone* feels like regret: if things were as they should be, Richard (and Baldwin) could focus on "my own sense of life"—in other words, could just be an artist.

## Race and Modern Acting

Did Baldwin read Stanislavsky? It seems probable that he did: in his novel *Another Country* (published in 1962, two years before the premiere of *Blues*), *An Actor Prepares* is one of the books that Eric has lying around his house.[39] If he did read Stanislavsky, *Tell Me How Long the Train's Been Gone* is not only about Strasberg, but also about Strasberg's Russian progenitor; if he didn't, his clairvoyance is startling. Stanislavsky's early writings about his system, translated by Elizabeth Reynolds Hapgood as *An Actor Prepares* and published in 1936, open with an almost identical scene to the scene Baldwin sets up in *Tell Me How Long the Train's Been Gone* in Saul San-Marquand's workshop: an incompetent performance of Othello.

Stanislavsky's book tells the story of an acting company learning the Stanislavsky system from their new director, Tortsov, opening on their first day of class, when Tortsov instructs the young actors to go home and work on a scene playing any character in dramatic literature. Kostya, the first-person narrator, somewhat randomly chooses Othello. At home, he finds the costume and props he thinks the Moor would have: he tucks a paper-cutter in his belt like a dagger, wraps a towel around his head as a turban, makes a gown out of his sheets, and uses a dinner tray as a shield. But he is not satisfied: "Yet my general aspect was modern and civilized, whereas Othello was African in origin and must have something suggestive of primitive life, perhaps a tiger, in him."[40] Rehearsing again the next day, he smears chocolate cake on his face to make it black, and flashes the white of his eyes and teeth.

The description of Kostya's attempts to play a character of a different race takes up the first nine pages of the book. His struggles model the struggles of an actor without the tools of Stanislavskian "craft": he begins from externals, instead of interior logic; he is incapable of adapting what he had rehearsed at his home to the stage of the theater; he is self-conscious in front of an audience and feels he does not have the freedom he had at home. When he tries to get out of this rut and improvise the character off the text, he feels confused and out of control: "I did not control my methods; rather they controlled me."[41] When he begins to perform the scene for the class, he is more concerned about pleasing the audience than playing the character. Then he has a disastrous experience trying to do his own makeup, and is rescued by a makeup artist who "covered my whole face with a sooty shade, proper to the complexion of a Moor. I rather missed the darker shade the chocolate had contributed, because that had caused my eyes and teeth to shine." But again, when Kostya gets on stage, he is thrown off balance, and instead of the flashes of inspiration he expects, given what an excellent costume he has on, he finds he cannot do the scene without reverting to the ingrained habits and rhythms he had rehearsed. The only thing that seems to crack his superficial performance is a long discussion with his friend Leo of Othello's emotions, which Kostya has not even considered. When Leo leaves, and Kostya again goes over his part, he is emotionally moved as never before: "I almost wept."[42]

When his turn to perform arrives, Kostya has a curious experience. At first, on stage, he feels stage fright. Trapped in self-consciousness and unable to perform as he been able to alone in rehearsal, he freezes: "The effort to squeeze out more emotion than I had, the powerlessness to do the impossible, filled me with a fear that turned my face and hands to stone." But unexpectedly, his frustration transforms into something else: "I was making a failure, and in my helplessness I was suddenly seized with rage. For several minutes I cut loose from everything about me. I flung out the famous line 'Blood, Iago, blood!' "[43] In an instant, the character of Othello is brought to life by the actor's real emotion. It doesn't matter that his emotion (that of an actor frustrated with a bad performance) bears only tangential relation to the emotion of his character (the rage of the betrayed general). His performed emotion works as an empty signifier, ready to be filled with whatever the accoutrements of text and play-world provide. This is the only moment in Kostya's performance that succeeds.

It turns out that Tortsov found all the students' performances, including Kostya's, mechanical, contributions to what he calls "the art of

representation," as opposed to true art, which never imitates. He turns
to Kostya:

> You are an intelligent person, yet why, at the exhibition performance,
> were you, with the exception of a few moments, absurd? Can you
> really believe that the Moors, who in their day were renowned for
> culture, were like wild animals, pacing up and down a cage? The
> savage that you portrayed, even in the quiet conversation with his
> ancient, roared at him, showed his teeth, and rolled his eyes . . . You
> were tempted by the external appearance of a black man in general,
> and you hastily reproduced him without ever thinking about what
> Shakespeare wrote.[44]

Kostya didn't play a person, he played a stereotype; he didn't play inner
life, he played external appearance. And this external acting style, disconnected from both actual bodily experience and the given circumstances
of the play, is just as unacceptable when one is playing another race
as it is when one is playing a part "close" to oneself. For Stanislavsky,
theater that is real art, and not just entertainment, portrays human experience, not stereotypes or clichés. The example of Othello is so instructive
because nowhere do stereotypes become more obviously activated than
in the European's idea of "the external appearance of a black man in
general."

   Despite the major historical differences, Kostya's Othello provides an
intriguing counterpoint to the Workshop actor's Othello in Baldwin's
novel. In both Baldwin's novel and in Stanislavsky, the performance of
blackness is the litmus test for the white actor's ability to remain truthful while playing character: the paradox at the core of Stanislavskian
acting. In both cases, the actors fail, but, tellingly, they fail for nearly
opposite reasons. Whereas Kostya exoticizes and primitivizes Othello, the
Workshop actor brings the character so close to himself that he becomes
illegible. Stanislavsky's problem was getting the actor away from external theatrical clichés and toward the kinds of emotion that are universal
to humanity; Baldwin's problem is that this universalist mandate has
become what Cindy Patton calls "milquetoast humanism [that] promotes
tolerance, but understands tolerance to be the property of white, Christian males who use it to reestablish their position as the Universal from
which are distinguished the particulars who need to be tolerated."[45] Baldwin's novel throws down the gauntlet: racism cannot be overcome merely
by acknowledging our shared humanity. But this critique of universalism,
in both *Tell Me How Long the Train's Been Gone* and *Blues for Mister*

*Charlie*, is inconclusive: both the novel and the play reveal their author's uncertainty as to how to proceed without it. Instead, *Blues for Mister Charlie*, which breaks off as the black townspeople are about to march, leaves its audience with a political potentiality: perhaps new kinds of identification could lead to new kinds of alliances.

Chapter 4

✦

## *Blues* and *The Blacks*: Acting at the Close of Humanism

With *Blues for Mister Charlie*, Baldwin tried to write a play that was both realistic and politically galvanizing: that, *pace* Marx, adequately represented the world *and* tried to change it. One problem he ran into was how to treat his characters: how much should the characters represent individuals, conceived of psychologically, and how much should their individuality be subsumed to the representation of types?[1] Ultimately, Baldwin was ambivalent: he understood that group identification, understood to subsume individual identity, and its attendant fantasies are necessary for political action, but he was also melancholic about the erasure of individual uniqueness. This attention to the collective fantasies necessary for political action aligns Baldwin with another playwright to whom he is seldom compared, but should be: Jean Genet. Genet's play *The Blacks*, Bernard Frechtman's translation of *Les Nègres*, opened at the St. Mark's Playhouse in 1961, closed in New York just as *Blues* was opening, and unquestionably shaped the theatrical landscape in which *Blues* was received. The longest-running Off-Broadway play of the decade (it ran for over three years), *The Blacks* (which would have been called *The Niggers*, a more accurate translation, had Tennessee Williams not advised Frechtman against it) launched or cemented the reputations of some of the eminent black actors of that generation: Roscoe Lee Browne, James Earl Jones, Cicely Tyson, and Godfrey Cambridge, among others, like Maya Angelou (then Maya Angelou Make). Indeed, *The Blacks*, by all accounts, had a far greater impact in the United States than *Les Nègres* did in France.

Baldwin had known Genet since his time in Paris in the 1950s. (According to Edmund White, they both frequented the *Reine Blanche*, a gay bar in Saint-Germain whose name, the White Queen, appears as a central character in *Les Nègres*, a tantalizing biographical detail that raises questions about the play's structural and thematic relation to drag and gender performance.)[2] He frequently sat in on rehearsals for *The Blacks*: Maya

Angelou, who played a role, reported that "since Jimmy knew Genet personally and the play in the original French, nothing could keep him from advising me on my performance."[3] Amiri Baraka compared the two plays in a panel discussion of *The Blacks* on the occasion of its remounting by the Classical Theater of Harlem in 2003, critiquing the panel's premise: why are we here talking about *The Blacks*, a play written by a white Frenchman, Baraka asked, instead of Baldwin's *Blues for Mister Charlie*?[4] Indeed, by declaring in his 1987 eulogy for Baldwin, "As far as I'm concerned, it was *Blues for Mister Charlie* that announced the black arts movement," Baraka had already juxtaposed Baldwin's play to *The Blacks*, which some critics, if with reservations, have considered a launch point for black American theater.[5]

Whereas *Blues for Mister Charlie*, performed on Broadway by the famous Actors Studio, was received as mainstream American drama, *The Blacks*, performed at the tiny St. Mark's Playhouse, was understood to be an avant-garde experiment. But the parallels between *Blues* and *The Blacks* are revealing. Both plays are about a symbolic murder. Both plays, furthermore, use that murder to juxtapose several different levels of performance. In *The Blacks*, the internal performance of the murder of the "white woman" (she is played by one of the black characters), to be played as excessively theatrically as possible—to make no mistake that it is a ritual around a symbol—is juxtaposed to the real performance of the black actors for the white audience, on which Genet insists.[6] Also like *Blues*, *The Blacks* stages a trial, in which the outcome is a foregone conclusion. The crime in *The Blacks* is the murder of a white woman; by the end of the play, we learn that the trial is a ritual performed every night for the (real) white audience of the theater in order to distract them from the revolutionary war going on offstage, in which a traitor has just been executed. "The blacks" perform blackness and whiteness with equal theatricality, but Genet's point is not only that race is performance, but also that it is no less real for being so: ultimately, as Una Chaudhuri has argued, the play foregrounds the reality of racial conflict in the real confrontation going on in the theater between the black actors and the white audience.[7] Race may be constructed, but racial conflict is the reality of world politics.

Peter Brook, speaking in 1966, put it succinctly:

> I saw *The Blacks* in Paris, and I saw *The Blacks* in this theatre. In Paris, because of the political, racial situation, the play was completely theoretical: a rather pompous and boring overwritten piece of romantic theatre. Here I found it of extraordinary interest. I was

conscious that the performance I was at was necessarily different from the performance the night before, and the night after; that the proportion of black and white people in the audience conditioned all sorts of tensions coming to and from stage and audience . . . One's own feelings were fed and disturbed in this way; the play was continually shifting its position.[8]

Brook's comments corroborate Chaudhuri's argument that despite the play's exceptionally layered semiotic, its ultimate effect is not derealization but rerealization. The play takes the form of a ritual drama, which, we learn, happens every night, in which a black is put on trial by a "white" court (black actors in whiteface) for the rape and murder of a white woman. The play's *peripeteia* is the discovery that this ritual performance, the play within the play, has been designed by the blacks to hide from the real white audience (i.e., the audience in the theater) the real event: the trial and execution of a black traitor by the revolutionary black forces that have overthrown their white colonizers. This "real" event is never shown, and is only referred to obliquely by one character, Newport News, who appears and reappears to give news to the ritual performers of what is happening offstage.[9] The conflict between the two levels of performance gives the play what Chaudhuri calls its "semiotic theme." On the one hand, there is nothing outside the performance: the offstage trial is another level of signification. On the other hand, the play does assert a "real": the real racial conflict going on in the theater between the real black actors and the real white audience. Genet's play "puts the image back in the mirror and—after much metatheatrical derealizing and distancing—brings about a real confrontation between real people." Not "a fog of pseudophilosophical trivialities about the illusion of reality and the reality of illusion" (Chaudhuri), or a "rather boring and overwritten piece of romantic theater" (Brook), but the real relationship between the actors and the audience, in other words, the real praxis of the theater.[10]

What is so interesting, however, is that the real people who saw the New York production lamented exactly the fact that a real confrontation had not taken place. Norman Mailer, for instance, loved the play but nonetheless complained, in his *Village Voice* review, "How much real emotion and complexity we could have been given if a literal white had looked across the stage at a literal black." Mailer's review construes Genet's self-conscious theatricality as homosexual artificiality, linking the play's obfuscation to Genet's love of falseness, and this to the surrealist gesture of deflection, which blocks real communication. The problem with Genet, according to Mailer, is that he is both a great artist and "an unconscionable faggot, drenched in chi-chi." (This derision occasions a jab at Tennessee Williams: "that outer-Williams, ta-ta Tennessee, cry not that the French write it better than thee.") The play's homosexuality occludes its true force, the violent hatred of blacks for whites. For Mailer, the frame of the play is merely a distraction from the immediacy of this literal confrontation: "The foreground of 'The Blacks' is too oppressive . . . White and Black in mortal confrontation are far more interesting than the play of shadows Genet brings to it."[11]

The opacity that Mailer linked to homosexual cowardice and European surrealism, Lorraine Hansberry related, in her clear-eyed *Village Voice* rebuttal to Mailer's review, to romantic racism, which segregation renders inevitable: "We have been locked away from one another and, sadly, it is not really curious that we seem to throw such romantic shadows on the windows."[12] The play's "shadows," which Mailer read as gay artificiality, Hansberry reads as the erotic shadows cast by the "quaint notions of white men," which exoticize blacks just as racist stereotypes always have.[13] Referring to Genet and Mailer as "the new paternalists," she took issue with the play's portrayal of blacks as fundamentally different from whites: "Between the play and Mailer's discernible reaction to it, a duet was indeed sung . . . this is especially so in his lusty acceptance of the romantic racism which needed evocation to allow for the conceptualization of *The Blacks* in the first place." (Hansberry went on to write a rebuttal to *The Blacks* called *Les Blancs*, her own realist treatment of African decolonialization.) But despite their clear differences, Mailer and Hansberry came to some similar conclusions about the meaning of Genet's play in its American context: all those levels of performance—the blacks as "blacks" for the white court, the blacks as "whites" as the court, the blacks as "blacks" and "whites" for the white audience—distracted from the reality of racial conflict. The real problem with *The Blacks*, beyond the obviously offensive fact that here was a play about blacks written with brio by a white man, was the play's absolute abandonment of humanism and the mutual recognition that humanist theater supports. The "shadows" both she and Mailer decry in Genet's play are clearly the opposite of the light and vision of realism.[14]

Indeed, from its first moments, *The Blacks* attacks the idea that mutual recognition is possible or even desirable: the point of the play, as Archibald, the Master of Ceremonies, says early on, is to "increase the distance that separates us—a distance that is basic."[15] The theatrical frame of *The Blacks* highlights and even extends the distance between the actors and the audience; the white audience is deliberately prevented from identifying with the blacks on stage. But for Genet, this refusal of identification has a political point, which he underscores by dramatizing an emphatically pernicious instance of it, when the black character Virtue identifies with the White Queen as a response to her lover Village's declarations:

> VIRTUE (*softly, as if in a state of somnambulism*): I am the lily-white Queen of the West. Only centuries and centuries of breeding could achieve such a miracle! Immaculate, pleasing to the eye and to the soul! . . .
>
> (*The entire court listens attentively.*)
>
> Whether in excellent health, pink and gleaming, or consumed with languor, I am white. If death strikes me, I die in the color of victory. Oh noble pallor, color my temples, my fingers, my belly! Oh eye of mine, delicately shaded iris, bluish iris, iris of the glaciers, violent, hazel, gray-green, evergreen iris, English lawn, Norman lawn, through you, but what do we see . . .
>
> (*The Queen, who has finally awakened but is in a dazed state, listens to the poem and then recites along with Virtue*)
>
> . . . I am white, it's milk that denotes me, it's the lily, the dove, quicklime and the clear conscience, it's Poland with its eagle and snow! Snow . . .[16]

Virtue's performance of identification suggestively resonates with the kind of externally identified performance I discussed in my first chapter: hypnosis. When Virtue starts to speak with the Queen's voice, she does so "*as if in a state of somnambulism*," like a spiritualist medium or someone being hypnotized. The Queen, too, who was asleep, recites the litany of white beauty along with Virtue "*in a dazed state*"—the two, Virtue and the Queen, become one in extra-conscious communion. Virtue can accept being idealized as a love-object only if she somnambulantly identifies with whiteness. Here, hypnotic identification means the psychic interpolation into a racist aesthetic structure.

Genet presents another option for performance, however. In the midst of Virtue's hypnotic daze of whiteness, Felicity suddenly interjects. Her speech, in contrast to every other declamation in the play, is directed not to whites (the White Court and white audience) but to Negroes:

> (*Suddenly Felicity stands up. Everyone looks at her and listens in silence.*)

FELICITY: Dahomey! . . . Dahomey! . . . Negroes from all corners of
the earth, to the rescue! Come! Enter into me and only me! Swell
me with your tumult! Come barging in! . . . Giantess with head
thrown back, I await you all. Enter into me, ye multitudes, and be,
for this evening only, by force and reason.[17]

The Kingdom of Dahomey, in West Africa, was in the midst of fighting
for its independence when Genet wrote *Les Nègres*; it regained independence in 1959–60 (it is now the Republic of Benin) and was a powerful
symbol for African self-determination when *The Blacks* ran in New York.
In other words, unlike the pomp and satire of Archibald's ritual, and in
stark contrast to the baroque and creepy white-identified somnambulism
that has just occurred, this is a direct call to arms: a call to a group identification between Negroes on behalf of Negroes and Negro revolution—if
only "for this evening," if only in the theater. Felicity appeals once more
to political identification in the moment of suspense before Village has
to act out the ritual rape and murder, when again she stands up straight:
"Dahomey! Dahomey! To my rescue, Negroes, all of you! . . . Are you
there, Africa with the bulging chest and oblong thigh?"[18]

Felicity's speeches in some ways parallel Juanita's climatic speech in
*Blues for Mister Charlie*.[19] Both enact a nonpsychological—indeed, a cor-
poreal and sexual—identification-cum-incorporation ("enter into me")
alongside a revolutionary call to arms. Both deny that this identification
could or should be universal. Baldwin was more ambivalent about this
than Genet was, but this shift from "universal" psychological identification for the sake of state power—always already an identification with
whiteness—to separatist identification for the sake of political action is
key to both Genet and Baldwin's interventions. What complicates matters
concerning *The Blacks* is that, unlike Baldwin, Genet was avowedly not
interested in the political efficacy of art. He repeatedly refused, despite the
efforts of a diverse roster of interviewers, to relate his theater to politics,
a silence that appeared most strange in light of his frenzied political activ-
ism after 1968, during his collaborations with the Black Panthers in the
United States and the Palestinians in the Middle East.[20] In a characteristic
moment from 1970, during an interview with Michèle Manceaux about
his U.S. tour with the Panthers, when Manceaux asked if he would have
written *The Blacks* in the same way after his trip, Genet bristled at the
implied connection: "I don't think that Brecht did anything for communism, and the revolution was not set off by Beaumarchais's *The Marriage
of Figaro*. I also think that the closer a work of art is to perfect, the more
it is enclosed within itself."[21]

Furthermore, as commentators from Ossie Davis to Roscoe Lee Browne to Amiri Baraka have pointed out, the play seems to come to rest in a night-marish vision of postrevolutionary violence, with the offstage execution of the black traitor as a warning, perhaps, against too-optimistic views of African liberation, or perhaps suggesting, as Browne thought, that the play was about the essential corruption of humanity. But the traitor is not simply a victim of despotic violence. A recurrent figure in Genet's oeuvre, the traitor challenges the social order by confusing the terms of his identity and its identifications. In *Prisoner of Love*, Genet writes of the ecstasy of betrayal as implicit in the desire to translate the other, the desire at the root of writing: betrayal as the result of the interpenetration of bodies and beliefs.[22] Betrayal is a kind of identification–anti-identification, identification barred.

In *The Blacks*, the traitor never appears on stage, but he structures the drama: it is his trial and execution we are being distracted from with the ritual and show trial on stage. His execution, ostensibly the play's climax, is not only absent from the stage but even removed from the world off-stage: to signify it, Genet's stage directions instruct firecrackers to explode offstage, their sparks visible through the curtain, making clear that we the audience were not privy to even a hint of the real thing. The fireworks act as another distraction from the pure negativity of the absent traitor. Later, Genet would write that "the essence of theatre is the need to create not merely signs but complete and compact images masking a reality that may consist in the absence of being. The void."[23] The absent traitor is the void behind the mask of theatrical images, and just like the erasure of Richard in *Blues for Mister Charlie*, his martyrdom in *The Blacks* is treated with ambivalence: is the society that martyrs the reminders of our noniden-tity destroying what might possibly save us from the trap of fixity, or is this martyrdom necessary to maintain collective identity? Genet had ideas about these problems, despite his (rather theatrical) insistence that art had nothing to say to politics. In *Prisoner of Love*, he muses on whether the Black Panthers accepted him because they "recognized a natural sham":

> Is the event that shows someone for what he is a sort of epic eruption, a fleeting upsurge of depths, of hollows that people as well as indi-viduals shrink from admitting? Perhaps the abjectness of the natural sham lifts him high enough to be seen permanently sticking up out of the lava. Another freak of nature.[24]

The self is an "epic eruption"—this is subjectivity as orgasm. Personal reve-lation is not "truth," it's ejaculate. Genet's description of identification based on mutual recognition of "natural sham[s]," "freak[s] of nature," suggests a different kind of alliance than that built on identity. This is a dangerous alliance, always provisional, and always on the brink of disintegration.

## Strasberg vs. *TDR*

Allan Francovich, writing in the *Tulane Drama Review* in 1969, offered a blunt diagnosis of *The Blacks*' confused reception:

> An acting tradition based on Stanislavski has taught us to look for dramatic meaning on the surface of the play, in motivation, character, plot, and style. In a play as involuted as *The Blacks*, the meaning does not reside in surface articulations. It is embedded in deeper theatrical relationships, between actor and audience, between the ritual and political dimensions of the text.[25]

How could "an acting tradition" be blamed for a public's inability to understand a play? Francovich's article reveals how powerful that "acting tradition" had become, and how intimately the rejection of it was bound up in the ethos of 1960s avant-garde theater. His essay charts a transformation of theatrical values: no longer will American theater makers, if they think themselves avant-garde, rely on the "surface" elements of motivation, character, plot, and style; rather, they will work with the "deeper theatrical relationships" between actor and audience, ritual and politics. If Francovich's terminology, in his diagnosis of the hermeneutic problem *The Blacks* engendered, remained generic, other critics and artists were less obscure about whose method in particular they rejected. According to Herbert Blau, reflecting on the era a few decades later, "virtually all" of the theater groups aligned with the New York avant-garde of the 1960s and 1970s had "considerable disdain for the tradition of acting . . . taught by Lee Strasberg at the Actors Studio." Blau attributes this disdain to "an anti-humanist critique that—with certain mixed feelings, to be sure—could look on the acting even of a Marlon Brando or a Kim Stanley or a Geraldine Page as if it were the apotheosis of individualism turned utterly solipsist."[26] The New York production of *The Blacks* coalesced this critique that was at once aesthetic, philosophical, and political. By the late 1960s, Method acting was the line drawn in the sand of twentieth-century American performance, with mainstream theater on one side, and avant-garde theater on the other. *The Blacks* and the controversy around it reveal, as did Baldwin's *Blues for Mister Charlie*, the extent to which the political context of the civil rights struggle and the conversation and dissent it catalyzed was a crucial vector of pressure against the rigidity of Method acting's model of the American subject.

The year 1964 was transformative for New York theater. In January, as *The Blacks* was rounding out its third year at the St. Mark's Playhouse, Adrienne Kennedy's *Funnyhouse of a Negro* went up at the East End Theater; in March, just one month before *Blues for Mister Charlie* made its debut on Broadway, LeRoi Jones / Amiri Baraka's *The Dutchman* went up at the Cherry Lane. Also in 1964, a particularly damning article appeared in the *Tulane Drama Review*: Rogoff's "Lee Strasberg: Burning Ice," with which I began the second half of this book. It came at the end of the second of two issues *TDR* devoted to Stanislavsky, which together chart a striking reversal of values. The first issue opened with Theodore Hoffman's critical but admiring article "Stanislavsky Triumphant," and included contributions from Lee Strasberg (interviewed by Richard Schechner), as well as Stella Adler, Sanford Meisner, and others. The second issue, published in the winter, opened with a note by editor Richard Schechner called "Twilight of the Gods" that resembles nothing so much as a eulogy, in which he both chides and offers thanks to elders of the Group Theatre generation, including Strasberg and Kazan, but, as his title announces, declares their relevance over.[27] But Rogoff's article is the showstopper, condemning Strasberg as a con artist and a dictator, a Svengali, a Stalin, and a J. Edgar Hoover all at once: "Strasberg's underground message . . . is a smoothly meshing network composed of studied omissions, marketplace values, darkly inspired insecurities, and downright spiritual paralysis."[28] Strasberg fought back with a defensive letter to the editors of *TDR*, but the battle lines were clear: the title of the published letters reads "Strasberg vs. *TDR*."[29]

## The Method and the Margins

> You watch apprehensively—as you did Martin Scorsese's *Raging Bull*, which Bobby De Niro played. In the company of those performers you should not feel safe, any more than you do walking through a Harlem slum street at night if you're white, or driving over an African savannah in an open jeep as the sun sets and the predators begin to stir.
>
> —Elia Kazan, *A Life*

In writing this revisionary history, I have not only challenged dismissive views of Method acting but also mined what the Method itself repressed.

Elia Kazan's analogy, in his autobiography, between the sense of danger that a great actor should incite and the danger of a Harlem street or an African plain, stages a poignant return of this repressed that reveals much about the racial circumference of Method acting's repudiations. Joseph Roach, in *Cities of the Dead*, demonstrates how the strategic occlusion of the black racial other, on whose bondage the American and European notions of liberty depend, returns paradigmatically in performance, the medium in which the dead cannot help but reappear.[30] Method acting attempted to harness the danger of what Roach calls "surrogation" by staging the return of the past in personal, subjective terms. But it is telling that Kazan's description of the true actor (Robert De Niro, the paradigmatic Method actor of the second generation) relies on the "Harlem slum street," the "African savannah," phantasmatic sites of domestic and international colonialism.[31] *The Blacks* stages this alignment between the "dangerous" spaces in which whites are not in control and the dangerous space of the theater. Genet brought front and center what Kazan's description suppresses: in his play, the actor's nonbeing that "haunts and taunts" the social structure (as Samuel Weber describes theatricality) is fundamentally related to the black "nonbeing" that returns in the act of its refusal.[32]

"Performances tend to reveal," Roach writes, "whether the performers intend to or not, the intricately processual nature of relationships of difference."[33] Kazan's description suggests that he was not blind to the figure-ground relationship that spotlights the actor while obscuring the absent bodies on which his presence depends: "In order for performers to enact the strength and stability of the center, they must boldly march to the boundaries to reconnoiter," just as the Method actor must, in Kazan's imaginary, harness the power of the Harlem streets.[34] Kazan, however, could apparently conceive of those Harlem streets only as the thrilling, threatening margins of the theatrical center. Through the 1960s, even as the efforts of African American theater artists rendered American theater's exclusion of black experience increasingly impossible to ignore, the theorists and interpreters of Method acting never took on its implications for performers excluded from its brand of American universalism. In St. Mark's Church on what was then the Lower East Side—very much, in the early 1960s, outside the theatrical center of New York—*The Blacks* installed itself as a "monstrous double" (Roach) of theatrical humanism. Kazan's comment exposes why *The Blacks* presented such a challenge to a Method that could not conceive of the "Harlem slum street" except as a term of incorporative repression.

# Part Three

✦

*Methods and Scripts*

Chapter 5

✦

# "Come On, Alice, Stop Acting!"
# Scriptedness and the Radical Method

Accounts of modernist and avant-garde performance rarely if ever include Method acting, which, for some of the reasons I explored in the previous chapter, artists and scholars have long considered to be opposed to the avant-garde unraveling of the "seams joining drama to script to theater to performance," and aligned with the "illusionistic mimetic theater [that] is based on hiding the seams."[1] This chapter argues the opposite. Even as it relied on plays and play scripts, Method acting took part in the modernist critique of the primacy of the dramatic text and developed strategies for overcoming its perceived inadequacies. This is more intuitively grasped when one considers Method acting's impact on experimental film, where it directly inspired American experiments in improvisatory, actor-generated dialogue and direct cinema and *cinema verité* aesthetics.[2] But if calling Stanislavsky a modernist may no longer raise eyebrows, calling American Method acting modernist contradicts a half-century of conventional wisdom, which has taught us that Method acting exemplifies the conservative aesthetics of the early Cold War period. For me, asserting that Method acting is modernist means that we can begin to look beyond these stereotypical formulations and see its overlap with such contemporaneous American late modernist phenomena as Jackson Pollock's abstract expressionism, Anne Sexton's confessional poetry, and John Cassavetes's and Shirley Clarke's independent films. This chapter will suggest one direction that such an analysis could take and will put forward one artist whose work demonstrates its efficacy, William Greaves.

This chapter also reverses a teleology that despite recent efforts, particularly those of Martin Harries, is still too often taken for granted—*from* theater *to* film—to explore what the media of film and television can tell us about the medium of drama. An analysis of the relationship between Method acting and drama must take into account its relation to film: its popularization through Kazan's film directing, its relation to aesthetic shifts in film production, and its cinematic iconography, as well as the abundance of film scholarship on Method acting, which has embraced it as an object of inquiry far more than theater studies has. Harries's insights into theater and media, and particularly into the ways that theater artists responded to the rise of film, are therefore highly suggestive for an analysis of Method acting, a practice that is at least partially defined by its crossing of medial boundaries.[3] This chapter puts these two directions—Method acting's textual resistances and its relation to the rise of film as a performance medium—together. The crux I call "scriptedness," which refers not only to the dramatic text as such but to conventions, norms, and preordained behavioral and psychic structures to which authentic, immediate experience could be opposed, and was opposed, both in the overlapping discourses of the 1960s avant-garde and the New Left and by Method acting—with different results.

I conclude my argument about scriptedness with an analysis of William Greaves's fascinating, too-little-known 1968 experimental documentary *Symbiopsychotaxiplasm Take One*, one of an important group of American independent films that expanded the theories and practices of Method acting into a holistic aesthetics of the medium.[4] In addition to his long career as a documentarian, which included seminal film and television documentaries about African diasporic and African American experience, Greaves was a longtime member of the Actors Studio who taught acting at the Lee Strasberg Theater Institute from 1969 to 1982 and shared the Studio's 1980 Eleanor Duse Award.[5] Greaves's film pushes forward some of Method acting's most compelling elements, thematizing the resistance to scriptedness as both an aesthetic and a political problem and suggesting that Method acting might provide a unique way of dealing with it. Greaves's radical Method, on view in *Symbiopsychotaxiplasm Take One*, is up to the task of negotiating the blurry boundaries between performance and its others.[6]

## *Where's Daddy?*: Authenticity and Mediation

In William Inge's last Broadway play, *Where's Daddy?*, which premiered in 1966 in a Broadway production directed by Harold Clurman and starring Barbara Dana and Beau Bridges, Method acting is the subject of parody. Clurman had broken with Strasberg, his former friend and collaborator at the Group Theatre, years earlier, and Inge's play not only paints an ironic picture of the Method actor, but also articulates many of the cultural fault lines around which the Method's many controversies gathered. In *Where's Daddy*, Tom, a young, struggling actor, and Teena, his nineteen-year-old pregnant wife, are paragons and parodies of their generation: they live like bohemians, in a squalid flat, across the hall from a young intellectual Negro couple; they are aggressively and self-consciously different from their "retrogressive" parents; and they are passionately devoted to psychoanalysis. When the play opens, they have decided to break up and to give their baby up for adoption, because they are too "emotionally immature" and need to "find themselves." Teena seems ambivalent about this from the beginning, but for Tom, it's not just a generational but a vocational imperative. As he puts it to his former guardian, a dandified professor evocatively named Pinky,

> TOM: It's like this. I feel I'm a very good actor. My teacher thinks so, too. He tells me he thinks I can have a very notable career in the theater after I . . . [*sic*] find myself . . . I have to be *true* to myself.
>
> PINKY: That's all part of that awful "method" you go around preaching, isn't it?
>
> TOM: (*Staunchly.*) It's what I believe, Pinky.[7]

Devoted to the tenets of Method acting, Tom believes that he must "be *true*" to himself to be a good actor, while Pinky, in contrast, waxes nostalgic for a theatricality of self-transcendence: "In my day, actors played parts. They didn't play themselves. They didn't want to play themselves. They wanted to play the farthest thing from themselves they could find . . . You all think you have to be sordid to be real."[8] This is the image of the Method actor that has prevailed since the early days of the Actors Studio: the ripped T-shirt Brando-as-Stanley-Kowalski imitator, whose macho inarticulateness and emotional (and sometimes physical) nakedness demonstrate his authenticity.

Today we tend to read the imperative toward authenticity as either nativist chauvinism (what Aamir Mufti describes as "the impulse of authenticity towards the extermination of difference, on the one hand, and social self-destructiveness, on the other")[9] or naive individualism, easily dismantled by our sophisticated awareness of performativity, the constructedness of identity, and plural, intersectional selfhood. But in the 1950s and 1960s authenticity was a potent concept for Left intellectuals, as Martin Jay has argued, a trend epitomized by Marshall Berman's *The Politics of Authenticity*, from 1970, which declared that "the idea of authenticity . . . articulated men's deepest responses to the modern world and their most intense hopes for a new life in it."[10] Berman traces the desire for authenticity back to Rousseau and the Enlightenment, but Jay reads its New Left valorization as a more nationally specific concept: "the culmination of the powerful impact on American culture of Sartrean existentialism, which reinforced native inclinations, stemming from certain strains of evangelical Protestantism and the frontier experience, to rely on individual responsibility to resist external conformist pressures."[11] Jay's description is consistent with many sketches of the "native inclinations" that produced Method acting, like that of David Krasner, who argues that the association of Method acting with gritty realism is "due in part to an emphasis on what in America counts as authenticity . . . [which] helped mediate the individual's claim to a national sense of self ."[12] Jay's reference to existentialism also links back to certain strains of Method acting, especially Kazan's version, with its emphasis on individual choice and decision, and to the commonplace association of Method acting with existentialism as an intellectual fashion (the 1957 *Saturday Evening Post* article that did much to popularize a certain image of the Method actor confided that Actors Studio members "can discuss the theories of Existentialism readily").[13]

As Jay notes, one important dissenting voice against the proauthenticity chorus of midcentury thought belonged to Theodor Adorno, whose *The Jargon of Authenticity*, published the same year Inge's play was written (1964), is a scathing critique of the ideology of authenticity (and of existentialism more generally). Although it was written for a German audience, Adorno's book is suggestive for an analysis of Method acting, not only because it sheds light on a critique that we now often take for granted, but also because of its repeated articulation of that critique in terms of performance and mediation. What Adorno calls out in the ethical jargon of German existentialism (in addition to its pseudo-religiosity, complicity with capital, and denial of history—all charges that have attended Method acting) is its promise of *immediacy*: its faith in experiences—"encounters," "statements," and so on—that escape or transcend mediation.[14] As an eminent example of the jargon, Adorno cites a description of a TV program in which the author recounts with awe the experience of watching a preacher on television: "Thanks to the noble humane power of conviction that radiated out from him," the authenticity-mad author writes, "not only did his words, which were testified to by his pictorial presence, become completely credible, but the listener totally forgot the mediating apparatus."[15] It presents itself as intimate, honest, the opposite of conformist, depersonalized mass communication: "The jargon pretends that, as a close-at-hand manner of communication, it is invulnerable to humanized mass communication—which is precisely what recommends it to everyone's enthusiastic acceptance."[16]

Jay asserts that Adorno found the basis for this critique in an essay he is better known for quarreling with, Walter Benjamin's "The Work of Art in the Age of Mechanical Reproduction," which describes authenticity as "a function of reproduction, not a quality of what precedes it."[17] Indeed, Martin Harries has recently traced the debates in performance studies around theater's "presence" to this subtle argument in Benjamin's essay, that the presence and authenticity of the auratic art work is something that appears in retrospect.[18] That authenticity as an ethical value rises to social and cultural prominence in the context of technological reproducibility as a nostalgically imagined presence (like aura) is suggestive for an analysis of Method acting, whose techniques were intended to produce authentic emotion and truthful behavior, and which gained ascendancy along with the rise of film and television.[19]

*Where's Daddy?* lends credence to this interpretation, ironizing Tom's authenticity fetish, his cleave to an imagined theater, and juxtaposing it to the actual ubiquity of television and film as the contemporary actor's bread and butter. The curtain rises on Tom studying the script of a TV commercial, the only kind of acting job he can find:

TOM: "Gee, Coach, you're not putting me on, are you?" (*Pause.*) "I'm beginning to think you've got something, Coach."

TEENA: (*Interrupting.*) All your socks are washed.

TOM: (*Without looking up.*) I'm beginning to wonder why they turn away from me on the dance floor, Coach.

TEENA: You'll probably have to do them yourself after you leave. It's really very simple. Just remember to get one of those new hardwater soaps on the market. One brand's as good as another. Just put a tablespoonful in a sinkful of water and let them soak for three minutes.

TOM: Sounds like another commercial.[20]

Teena's practical domestic instructions sound to Tom "like another commercial," a sign of canned, pre-scripted domestic conventionality that he must resist. To counter it, Tom imagines an authentic theater in which he would reveal his true self: as Teena explains to her mother, "With commercials, it's different. They're not important. But Tom is very particular about the type of part he does in a play, and the type of director he works with."[21] A 1949 letter to Elia Kazan from more than thirty members of the Actors Studio in response to a *New York Times* editorial he published decrying the loss of New York theater buildings to radio and film confirms that even over a decade earlier, Method actors shared Tom's perspective on the moral difference between the media: "We share with you a feeling of alarm," they wrote to Kazan, "at the oppressive drive toward thought-controlled conformity. The 'nightmarish' unemployment situation among theatre workers is growing with the swallowing up of theatres by radio and television." "Thought-controlled conformity" is conflated with the "swallowing up" of theater by mass media, which is totally opposed to real theater and real civic culture: "We agree completely that the preservation of the theatre is a 'civic matter' and believe that this would be a happier country with less B-36s and more culture."[22]

What *Where's Daddy?* also demonstrates, however, is that Method acting's ethic of authenticity should be considered not only a reaction to the new media of film and television—the work of acting in the age of mechanical reproduction—but also to its adversarial relationship with acting's original mediation: the dramatic text. If authentic theater stands against technological reproducibility, what happens to the reproducible script? In this first scene, the "kitchen sink" realist drama is deauthenticated and debased by its contact with television: Inge's play suggests that the scriptedness of the dramatic script comes into focus as such after the commercial scripts of film and television have made scriptedness itself seem like a problem. In *Where's Daddy?*, the problem is the multiplication and contagion of the television script, which infects the script of the domestic scene: when Teena's lines about soap and Tom's lines about deodorant ring similar, scriptedness is suddenly everywhere. Inge even includes a corresponding jab at his frenemy Tennessee Williams, when Teena's mother refers to a particularly violent scene from *Suddenly Last Summer* as a scene from a Disney movie.[23] The performer's authenticity is not only a nostalgic construction after film, but a construction, in some sense, after text—after the texts of modernist drama shifted the focus of theater away from the work of the actor toward the work of the playwright. The Method actor's authenticity was not only a consolation after reproducible media destroyed the actor's aura; it was also a consolation for the loss of the position of the actor as the primary artist of the theater.

As I argued in my introduction, Method acting's relationship to text was conflicted: on the one hand, the Actors Studio, which described itself as dedicated to "the union of actor and playwright," remained focused on plays over and against the tide of avant-garde theater, and both Strasberg's own writings and the tape-recorded Studio sessions abound with dramaturgical commentary. On the other, Strasberg is famous for declaring that the words are secondary to the character's emotional journey.[24]

Nor was this ambivalence unique to Strasberg: it had already been articulated in Elia Kazan's speech on the occasion of the Studio's founding in 1947. Describing his contemporaneous work directing Tennessee Williams's *A Streetcar Named Desire*, Kazan recounts how he came to realize how a scene in the play, in which the leading man is called from a fight with his wife and her sister to a telephone call about his bowling team, should be interpreted. What appeared as a dramatic fracture ("even an irrelevancy") could be made whole with the right reading, intimately associated with the right performance:

> [The interruption] had to be read entirely as part of the scene with the women—and with direct dramatic reference to it. The import of the speech was not in the writing, but in Acting.
>
> Did you ever try to tell this to a radio actor. And after having received his polite and earnest assent (Radio actors are always, always polite) did you ever try to get it out of him? . . . "Chum, its not [sic] in the reading."[25]

"It's not in the reading"—but it *is* in the reading: in how the scene "had to be read." The "Acting" that is the import of the scene is a form of textual interpretation, "a little examination." Kazan can't "get it out" of the too-polite radio actor, who fails to understand what the director means, because he and his mediating apparatus are too "polite" to capture the Acting epitomized later in this passage by Marlon Brando, trained to know his own impolite presence and use it to be impolite with the text, reading decision where there could only be "interruption," reading the violence in a seeming "irrelevancy." The impolite character and the impolite actor merge in a theatrical unveiling of the scene's unconscious aggression.

On the surface, this anecdote might seem an uncomplicated explanation of Stanislavskian through-line, connecting two seemingly unrelated dramatic incidents with a unified logic of character. Instead of "interruption," "irrelevancy," there is psycho-logic: this sounds like Stanislavsky's *Creating a Role*, which begins with a section on how to study and analyze a play and emphasizes the importance of mapping the inner logic of each part through a series of units and objectives, conscious and unconscious, small and large.[26] This is not just a unified interpretation, however, but an overcoming of a prior break: the break of the telephone call that interrupts the domestic scene. This intrusion of the outside is a verbal, not a physical action: the problem of the scene is that the telephone call is just words, independent of narrative significance. The actor's job is to

overcome this break of disembodied language introduced by the disembodied communication of the telephone. Of course the radio actor can't
do it: what's important is the physical presence that is impolite, authentic,
decisive, violent—and unmediated. Moreover, on this scene, the intrusion
of mediating words (words of the medium, words as the medium) must
be conquered by the imposition of a more powerful presence by being
combined with it. The machine, the telephone, collaborates with the Acting, which becomes visible in and through its mediation.[27]

Kazan's anecdote, while ostensibly articulating the power of the actor's
assertion, instead offers technological mediation a kind of détente: the
mediating apparatus (here the telephone, but one inevitably imagines Brando in the film version of *Streetcar*, his body overwhelming
the screen) can stay as long as the acting ("Acting") is more powerful.
Kazan's description thus aligns Method acting with the Benjaminian film
actor, who fights the filmic apparatus and wins, modeling for the modern
viewer how to prevail over the encroaching machination of work and
life.[28] However, here it is not that the actor's labor compensates for the
loss wrought by technology; rather, his labor, figured here as a piercing
psychic and physical aggression, is what makes the technological interruption, and the scene itself, meaningful.

*Where's Daddy?* comes to us from the other side of this compensatory
optimism: the actor, here, has no power to overcome the mediating apparatus's incursion, and all efforts to do so appear arrogant and naive. As
Inge makes clear, whatever his intentions, Tom can't escape scriptedness:
after all, his name itself, Tom Keen, was taken from a book (he picked
it "from some books I read at the orphanage"), as well as quoted, or
replicated, in the name of the deodorant brand he sells, Keenclean. Here
again, the television commercial is put on the same plane as literature,
as two faces of the scriptedness no one can evade. But if this pervasive
mediation feels like a problem to Tom, it certainly does not to Pinky,
who loves *I Love Lucy* as much as Milton. The play sides with Pinky:
choose a decent script (whether it's Milton or Lucille Ball) and you'll be
fine. For obviously Tom's halting self-knowledge is scripted too: he leans
obsessively on psychoanalytic jargon, unable to figure out what to say
without it. In *Where's Daddy?*, there's nothing between or beyond the
lines but silence. Toward the end of the play, signaling the seeds of his
newfound maturity, Tom reads from a different kind of script: Razz, his
neighbor, "sick of playing the angry black" (a stereotype no less canned
for being contemporary), has picked up *Othello* (another "angry black,"
of course), and Tom prompts him as he delivers Othello's description of
his success in wooing Desdemona with his rhetorical talents. (Of course,

Tom is also literally a script: Inge's.) And one of Pinky's last lines, as Tom finally comes home for good, is a quotation: "Shoulder the sky, my lad, and drink your ale." It's the final line from an A. E. Housman poem—and the title of a 1962 episode of the TV show *Route 66*.

Lest we conclude, however, that *Where's Daddy?* comes to rest in an abandonment of essentialism and a celebration of citationality and high–low cultural *mélange*, let us not forget the fundamental conservatism of the play's vision: making Tom a daddy, whether he likes it or not, is its raison d'être. The play may side with Pinky and Razz, but only after they have been shooed off the stage to allow Tom, Teena, and their baby to take their proper spotlight as the white American nuclear family of the future. Pinky's homosexuality may exempt him personally from that particular social responsibility, but the play still requires him to fight for its perpetuation. After all, Tom wanted to return to Pinky's protection and, Inge obliquely suggests, his former life as a rent boy (how exactly Pinky picked Tom off the street at age fifteen is left to the imagination—if it needs to be). And though the play mocks Tom's self-analysis of his own emotional immaturity, and the false guidance of Method acting and psychoanalysis, maturation and personal guidance toward greater self-knowledge are what the play itself gives Tom: in the end, he realizes his true love for Teena and takes on his "authentic" role as father.

### *Symbiopsychotaxiplasm* and the Radical Method

It starts like a normal film. A woman in a floral dress runs down the stairs under a footbridge in a park, pursued by a man in a suit calling her name, "Alice! Alice! Wait a minute!" He catches up with her and grabs her arm. "Just how stupid do you think I am?" the woman asks. But something is off: the sound quality is poor and her voice is shrill, and in the background, ambient static hasn't been filtered out. More: the woman is stiff, her attention is unfocused, she waits one second too long before responding. Her affects seem forced, and incompetently forced at that: a faint smile plays on her lips at one point, erroneously, and when she furrows her brow it seems almost mechanical. Though her lines imply that she wants desperately to be left alone, she hangs around with no seeming desire to move. "Come on, Alice, stop acting!" the man says, and when she turns around ("Don't touch me!"), we are suddenly looking at a close-up of another man's face, delivering the lines we have just heard: "Come on, Alice, stop acting." The screen splits: on the right, the second man's face; on the left, the face of a second woman, delivering the same lines as the first, but with a totally different intonation. She is crying and almost shaking, as the camera pulls in tightly around her mouth. The content becomes clearer: they are a couple, and the woman is confronting the man with her knowledge of "him, yes, him—some little faggot boy that half the world knows about." Just as this turn has been revealed, the scene cuts again: this time it's a full shot of a third woman's face, older than the other two. The dialogue becomes increasingly histrionic: "Believe in me." "Believe in you, how the hell can I believe in you, you've been killing my babies one after another!" As the scene goes on, we return to the split-screen, except this time both actors are in both shots, which show them from different angles.

The same park, the same script, but different actors—the same setup, the same circumstances, but different faces, different affects, different interpretations. "Come on Alice, stop acting," the man repeats; "how much of a phony can you be," one of the women shoots back—but it's clear that they are acting, that they are being phony, if to different degrees and with different effects. None of it is "convincing"; we can't "believe" in either the man or the woman—these are failed performances. As the third scene progresses, the "script" gets more arbitrary and more ridiculous, feeling less and less scripted, and more like the actors are making it up as they go along, with pseudo-psychological jargon: "Do you know what you're doing, that you keep, you keep saying these things to me, alright, about faggot, you're projecting, Alice, because you're trying to see in me things you see in yourself!" We hear a strange noise—the whine of audio equipment feeding back. Then, as the actors reach their climax ("Fuck *you*!"), the scene cuts to a shot of a neatly dressed older white woman and a shirtless young white man watching a film crew, around whom the camera pans. They are encircling a black man in a green mesh shirt, who is listening with headphones to the equipment's whine. "That's dreadful. This is terrible. Is that what we've been getting all the time? That's dreadful!" Jazz drumming cuts in, providing, with the whine, the soundtrack, as the title sequence begins.[29]

William Greaves's groundbreaking work of experimental cinema, *Symbiopsychotaxiplasm Take One*, shot in 1968 and amended with a second installment in 2003, defies categorization. Though the film is a documentary, its subject is a fictional pretext that is also a pretext about fiction: a fictional film that Greaves told his crew they were producing in New York's Central Park, while simultaneously turning the cameras back on them and shooting the shoot itself. The film alternates between a fictional drama, which Greaves calls "Over the Cliff," filmed with different pairs of actors but mostly with Patricia Ree Gilbert and Actors Studio mainstay

Don Fellows; the crew's disorganized efforts to film it; many disparate images and scenes of bystanders in the park, some of whom watch quietly, some of whom intrude, and some of whom pay no attention and apparently do not know they are being filmed; and, most compellingly, a secret meeting the crew had without Greaves. The larger film, which centers around the crew's anxious rebellion from Greaves and his chaotic direction, draws parallels between the fictional film shoot and the political crises of its era, as the surrounding realities of the shoot continually intrude on the frame, finally overtaking it entirely in the agitated political aria of a Central Park denizen who spontaneously approaches the set. In *Symbiopsychotaxiplasm Take One*, the controlled fiction is overtaken by its uncontrollable context. But in contrast to what one might expect— that the artificial script of "Over the Cliff" is meant to throw into relief the authenticity of Greaves's documentary—Greaves in fact challenges those very distinctions, between the unscripted and the scripted, reality and performance, authenticity and mediation.[30]

The inadequacy of the script becomes an issue early on in the film, in the crew's first secret meeting, in which they discuss the film and complain about Greaves's direction. What first appears to be a rebellion from the mandated hierarchy of the film shoot is almost immediately revealed to be something else:

> CREW MEMBER (JONATHAN GORDON): We were sitting around the other night and we, in talking, a few of us we realized that here is an open-ended film, with no plot that we can see, with no end that we can see, and an action that we can't follow. We're all intelligent people, the obvious thing is to fill in the blanks, to create for each of our own selves a film that we understand, and if we try to think about the reasoning of the director for allowing us the opportunity to do this, giving us the circumstances that enable us to be able to sit here, we can only conclude, at least we did last night, that he wanted it like this.[31]

The meeting, supposedly spontaneous, subversive, a break from the scripted, is, instead, a setup: part of the director's plan, part of the grand design of the film. Their conspiracy against authority is in fact a capitulation to it. Gordon's instinct was right: Greaves did want them to challenge his authority—and, clearly, he chose to include their meeting in his final cut of the film. As he reported later, he wanted to see how long it would take them to rebel from his incompetent direction: "The question was, 'when will they revolt?' When would they question the validity, the wisdom of doing the scene in the first place?"[32] Greaves saw this as a metaphor for politics: how absurd do the rules have to be before people revolt against them? The absurdity here is not only Greaves's halting uncertainty and sometimes outright incompetence as a director (or rather, his pretended incompetence, in his role as director), but also that of the scripted scene itself, with which the film began. However, this first glimpse at the crew's secret meeting also immediately rebukes the notion that there will be easy ways to escape the scripted, no matter how hollow, how bankrupt, it has become.

As the crew quickly articulates, the written scene of "Over the Cliff" is analogous to the roles scripted for men and women by society: predetermined, banal, pathetic, and no longer convincing. That the scene is poorly written makes its inadequacy all the more obvious:

> CREW MEMBER (BOB ROSEN): It's not like Edward Albee. I mean Edward Albee writes *Who's Afraid of Virginia Woolf?* and George and Martha are superdramatic people given lines that are brilliant lines . . . This is bad writing. This script is not good writing . . .
>
> VOICE (*off-camera*): On the other hand, human life isn't necessarily well written, you know.
>
> CREW MEMBER (JONATHAN GORDON): That's the whole point. Here we're confronted with one of the ultimate banalities of life. A pair of actors says this ultimate banality. Bill has given them these lines to say in the first place and um, tells them how to say it, um, and the actors try to find the meaning in it. Now I see it this way. I see every American man at some time in his life saying these lines at some time to every American woman . . . It's almost as if these lines were planted in their head when they were born.

Rosen cites Albee, and not Mike Nichols, the director of the film version of Albee's play: Albee's writing is the point. Serious drama, with "brilliant lines," appears, as theater did in *Where's Daddy?*, as an idealized counter to the triteness of the present script. This very banality points to its intractability in the national psyche: the lines "planted" in the heads of American women and men—scriptedness is no longer "brilliant lines" for "super-dramatic people," it is "one of the ultimate banalities of life." Following this script is not just a sign of what we now call normativity, and what in the 1960s was called conformity, but of uniformity: a nightmare of nonindividuation. Uniformity, not conformity—actually being the same, not just acting the same—is what Abigail Cheever has argued was the real nightmare behind the midcentury imperative toward authenticity.[33]

That the narrative content of "Over the Cliff" is so similar to the content of *Where's Daddy?* is telling: in both, a man seeks to escape the responsibility of a wife and child; in both, that escape is represented as an escape toward or into homosexuality (as the commonplace homophobia of mid-century psychology would have it, a sign of immaturity). Moreover, in both, homosexuality is the instigator of debased, feminized theatricality—phoniness and histrionics, in "Over the Cliff," and camp, in *Where's Daddy?*—while authentic theater is an unreachable masculine ideal of honesty and truth. In *Where's Daddy?*, Tom must learn to reject both his dream of an authentic theater and the homosexual escape represented by Pinky and to accept his normative social role (father), which is structural and therefore cannot be false, no matter how he feels about it. *Symbiopsychotaxiplasm Take One* takes a different view, ironizing Inge's conclusion: there is no "happy" resolution to the canned conjugal drama; there are also no children ("you've been killing my babies one after another!") to reify the structural continuity of the narrative and release the characters from the burden of charting new paths. (Interestingly, in *Who's Afraid of Virginia Woolf?*, there is also emphatically no child, just the fictional, fantasized son George and Martha have made up, whom George cruelly "kills" during the play.) Instead, there's "no end we can see, and an action we can't follow"—the roles that were once part of a coherent whole, a meaningful narrative, no longer make sense—and neither Alice nor Freddie can "stop acting," either in the internal fiction of the scene or in the film itself. Their roles don't work, but they're stuck inside them.

This is why it's so important to dismantle the script they've been given:

GORDON: You haven't been here for eight days and listened to this sordid, horrible conversation over and over and over again—with black faces, white faces, tall ones, old ones, young ones, skinny ones. You know? Convincing ones, unconvincing ones.

GREAVES: All right, all right, all right, so what else can we do? We've got all this equipment lying around here . . . It would be interesting—it really would be, Jonathan, it would be very interesting to see you surface with a better script . . . a better script as a screen test for a pair of actors.

GORDON: The way to make the script better is to, first of all, drop the euphemisms. You talk real language . . . Freddie has a cock, Alice has a cunt, Freddie likes or doesn't like to fuck Alice . . . That's the way to talk, and that's the way people, uh, can liberate themselves to talk about themselves, about what they really feel.

Are these really the only alternatives: the tired old script of "Over the Cliff," or "Freddie has a cock, Alice has a cunt"? Is that really the language that will liberate us?[34] Gordon's version of the script suggests a slangy (and simplistic) version of Herbert Marcuse's *Eros and Civilization*, that bible of the New Left, an alignment that also may explain some of Gordon and the other crew members' ambivalence around performance. In *Eros and Civilization*, performance denotes the inauthentic: the "performance principle," what Marcuse understands to be the contemporary version of the Freudian reality principle, represses the libido by sublimating it to socially useful, capitalistic behavior: "Libido is diverted for socially useful performances in which the individual works for himself only in so far as he works for the apparatus."[35] Performance is something you do for others in order to make them and yourself believe in it; performance presents an inauthentic self that supports the status quo. "Stop acting" is not just an interpersonal weapon: it's a political one.

But Greaves's film doesn't draw the same conclusions as Gordon—or perhaps it picks up where he leaves off. In the same conversation, Greaves responds to Gordon's challenge, and directly links the problem of the script to politics:

> GREAVES: The screen test proves to be unsatisfactory from the standpoint of the actors and the director and what happens is that the directors and the actor undertake to improvise something better than that which has been written in the screen test. This sort of palace revolt which is taking place is not dissimilar to the sort of revolution that's taking place, let's say, in America today. For instance, I represent the establishment, and I've been trying to get you to do certain things which you've become in a sense disenchanted with.[36]

Although Greaves in later years denied that his race had anything to do with his relationship with the crew, it is an unavoidable part of the film: the white crew members' relative unwillingness to directly criticize him contrasted with the blunt verdict of a vocal black crew member, "He doesn't know how to direct," seems partly a result of their unwillingness to see him as "the establishment." As film scholars Charles Musser and Adam Knee see it, Greaves was subverting "demeaning stereotypes of black ineptitude that haunt American cinema."[37] In another sense, Greaves's role is an acting job in and of itself: how does he need to behave to be seen as other than his prescribed role as a member of a marginalized minority? Can his performance surmount their habits of mind? And if not, if these habits are actually "planted in their minds when they're born," what good is a new script?

*Symbiopsychotaxiplasm Take One* suggests that Method acting might actually be equipped to deal with these problems, first because it acknowledges that they are problems: Method acting recognizes the impossibility of getting outside the scriptedness that it must nonetheless wrestle with, as well as the impossibility of fulfilling the command "Stop acting," and has developed techniques to deal with it. Rather than stabilize the authority of script and delimit the boundaries of characterization, rather than throw the script away and resort to Gordon's absurd example of plain speech, Method acting acknowledges the crisis of scriptedness: the crisis of the script's suddenly apparent, apparently incontrovertible, inadequacy. Its efforts to find the unscripted in the scripted—Rosen at one point refers to the moment "where you pass beyond that line of manipulation"—may not ultimately be successful (despite trying to "improvise something better," despite singing their lines as they do later, and despite using their own experiences, we never see the actors really nail the scene). But they are not naive, as they appear in Inge's play.

Greaves cites both Strasberg and Stanislavsky in his notes for *Symbiopsychotaxiplasm*, two of a motley list of influences that includes jazz, J. L. Moreno's psychodrama, Eisenstein's film theory, the second law of thermodynamics, Arthur Bentley's *An Inquiry into Inquiries*, the Heisenberg Uncertainty Principle, and Aurobindo on mysticism, before "Strasberg on acting," and "Stanislavsky on theater and acting."[38] This list is worth examining for several reasons: first, because it disrupts the context in which Method acting is usually placed, even the context in which I have placed it in this book. Instead of, say, Freud, HUAC, and Tennessee Williams—"the 1950s"—Greaves situates Method acting firmly within the ethos of "the 1960s": the avant-garde, empirical uncertainty, radical sociology, Eastern mysticism.

Second, the ideas on the list suggest a unique interpretation of Method acting that shifts its valences in surprising directions.[39] I have proposed that Greaves understood the acting theories of Stanislavsky and Strasberg to hold in tension the artificial and the real, the conventional and the—possibly mythical—impulses, affects, and emotional expressions that are outside convention, and many of the ideas on the list are similarly characterized by a tension between the structured and the unstructured: the melody and improvisation of jazz, Sri Aurobindo's material structuring of divine force.[40] Greaves's two hard science references, the second law of thermodynamics and the Heisenberg Uncertainty Principle, add a further wrinkle. The Uncertainty Principle—observation changes what is being observed—poses an implicit challenge to the absorptive model of realist performance: a "private moment" can never be the same if an audience is watching, and an actor's absorption is never complete. The Heisenberg principle poses a very different model for actor-audience relations than that posited by "fourth wall" naturalistic performance. Meanwhile, I read Greaves's interest in the second law of thermodynamics, which asserts the priority of entropy (and which also inspired Thomas Pynchon's contemporaneous *The Crying of Lot 49*), as a challenge to Diderot's model of acting, in which the actor's control, mental and physical, always has more power than her spontaneous sentiment—a model which, as Joseph Roach and others have argued, Stanislavsky maintained. Greaves shifts Stanislavsky and Strasberg's theories in a specific direction, away from closure, control, autonomy, and identity, and toward the spontaneous, the dynamic, and the relational.

Not identity, in other words, but identification: Greaves, the only artist in this book to write directly about Method acting and identification, understood it as an agonistic process, fraught with conflict and excitement: "Part of this strength, along with the excitement and challenge of this project, is *its basic conflict*, which is that of identification . . . identification of the actor with the part, the characters with each other, the actors with the crew, the crew with the script, with the actors, with the director, etc." (emphasis and ellipsis in original).[41] Identification, for Greaves, is multiple, heterogeneous, and contradictory; identification necessarily creates conflict. This is not the identification with racialized national norms that Baldwin and Genet deplored; it is closer to the disordered sexual identification of *Suddenly Last Summer*, but with a different thrust. Identification in this description is both psychic and political, a tactic of performance (the actor with the part), interpersonal psychology (the characters with each other), and group cohesion (the actors with the crew, the crew with the actors and the director), that overlaps, corresponds, or doesn't. Identification both separates and brings together, throwing groups and individuals into conflict, with each other and with themselves.

The title of Greaves's film comes from a term coined by the social theorist Arthur Bentley, who used the terms "symbiotaxis" and "symbiotaxiplasm" to describe the heterogeneous organisms, human and nonhuman, material, affective, and epistemological, that make up the world as we know it. In Bentley's writing, "symbiotaxis" takes the place of the binary of "individual" and "society," which he thinks inadequate to represent the intricate interweaving of bodies and behaviors that characterize *symbios*, life-together.[42] As a hermeneutic for Greaves's film, this compelling strain of Bentley's thought suggests that *Symbiopsychotaxiplasm Take One* proposes something other than what Eve Sedgwick, referring to Foucault, calls "the ruses of the repressive hypothesis," the unacknowledged persistence of the categories of repression and freedom, if often renamed as "hegemony" and "subversion," or, in this context, scriptedness and authenticity.[43] By inserting "psycho" in the middle of Bentley's term, Greaves makes his nondualism explicit: this is not about psychology as an individual, closed system, but about its intertwinement with the social, the experiential, the material. The actors, the crew, their habits, their psyches, their histories, their impulses: the symbiopsychotaxiplasm is a writhing mass of conflicts, identifications, actors, audiences, as heterogeneous and chaotic as Central Park itself. What's exciting—what's erotic (as Greaves remarks early on, perhaps teasing, perhaps not, sexuality is the real subject of the film)—is the way that these elements rub up against each other, the *symbio* (the life-together) with the *psycho*, the psycho with the *taxis* (the order, the arrangement), the taxis with the *plasm* (the material).

Mediation, in *Symbiopsychotaxiplasm*, is not an obstacle: it's a collaboration between disparate materials, working together to make something new. Nothing is purely immediate, purely spontaneous, but some things are new, are different, and that's exciting. Greaves's production notes articulate this excitement alongside his nonbinary thinking about scriptedness and unscriptedness: "Shoot a scene where they do a line reading. Have them improvise and 'put clothes on' the dialogue, which is naked . . . the kind of 'clothing' civilized people use to cover their psyches. Then let the dialogue as written explode."[44] This instruction implies the opposite of what the crew later complains: that the dialogue is pure convention and meaningless "euphemism," not "real language."[45] For Greaves, the dialogue is blank, naked: as he later explained, despite what was intended to be poor writing, "the actors will suddenly take hold and sometimes have a moment of truth, which takes what is purportedly bad writing and moves it to another level."[46] For Greaves, nakedness and truth are not the same thing; truth is the explosion of the written, its shards not destroyed but reorganized, moved "to another level." This is the point of all those Method exercises—not to strip away convention but to "explode" it.

It is fitting, then, that what is finally asserted in the film is a truth not *beyond* theatricality but in and with it. The film's final moments are devoted not to the crew's rebellion, which never really comes, nor to Gordon's "blunt" version of the script, nor even to the actors' rather ham-fisted attempts to feel something, but to the beautiful monologue of a homeless man who approaches the shoot. We meet him just after we've watched the actors trying to sing their lines, in an ambiguous parody of an Actors Studio exercise (Bob Rosen teases Greaves, "Is this what you do at the

Actors Studio?"). Greaves has just inquired, faux-innocently, whether the crew agrees that the singing might add some nice "texture" to the film, to which one of the quieter, disgruntled crew members growls, "There's no sense of reality." Suddenly there's a new voice in the background: "What is this thing? . . . oh it's a movie? So who's moving whom?" The camera pans across the park to where a small group of crew members has gathered around a man in a white shirt with his shoes slung over his shoulder. With dandyish intonation, with flamboyant gestures, Victor Vikowski (as he calls himself) makes everything that has come before him look canned:

> VICTOR: Merci beaucoup. Oh, you ain't got a cigarette?
>
> GREAVES: Merci beaucoup, that's French, isn't it?
>
> VICTOR: No, it's Jewish. Yeah, Jewish. Jewish, darling, very Jewish.

Victor's quick-witted answer to Greaves's condescension, claiming "merci beaucoup" for Jewishness, voices, with his camp delivery (prefiguring his later description of his sex life), the implicit semiotic chain linking abjection, homelessness, cosmopolitanism, Jewishness, and homosexuality.[47] As in Joseph Litvak's theory of "comicosmopolitanism," Victor is indeed "a happy pervert": instead of affirming the authority and priority of the film set over his home, the park, he disrupts the seriousness of that Art with comic mimesis: "Oh, what is this ABC *camera*?"[48] Victor is an artist too—as he tells the crew, he's a painter of watercolors—and his speechifying makes us wonder what scripts *they've* been following. Kicked out of his residential hotel for not paying his rent, Victor has been living in the park for the last nine weeks, but when Greaves tries to cast him as a philosopher of the park, he blanches: he's a graduate of Columbia University and studied architecture at Parsons School of Design. Despite this high culture past, Victor paints himself as an exemplary noncitizen, not hiding anything behind his educated vocabulary: "I made a drunk of myself there, but that's all right, at least it cleared my mind a little bit, because I hate bullshit, you know"; "I'm an alcoholic, by the way, too, you know; well, I am! I admit it, you know." Victor sees no need to dissemble, nor to explain his apparent contradictions.

Victor also delivers the only explicitly political speech in the film:

> VICTOR: We need changes. We all need money, true, but when you have to live off someone else's fucking back to make that buck, that's a penis of a dollar . . . When I see the Negroes and the Puerto Ricans and the whites pushing the wagons—I made a canvas just using blank-faced mannequins—because they manipulate

the business form. I know that scene, he's a big fat belly with a cigar smoking, you know, sitting back and "Ha ha!" Playing his horses and fucking a Puerto Rican or a colored girl in the back! I've seen the scenes, baby.[49]

He speaks with passion and conviction, but Victor is also clearly enjoying himself: acting out the "big belly with a cigar smoking," and delighting in his own elocution. He is far from Gordon's liberation from euphemism: "Freddie has a cock, Alice has a cunt." Instead, he makes use of "scenes": the downtrodden pushing wagons, the fat cat smoking a cigar. His speech would not be nearly as compelling were he not such a good performer, with bouts of stage-setting and character description. Victor renders the distinction between scripted and unscripted irrelevant. "This is what I call it," he repeats, "I coined that phrase"; he's not only written his own script, he's invented his own language. Is he making it all up? Is he "for real"? Does it matter? "I've seen the scenes, baby": for Victor, what is "seen" is "scene," and there's no other way of seeing.

In stark contrast to the roving camera of the rest of the film, the camera moves only slightly throughout this scene, which also seems unedited. It is almost as if a short stage play were suddenly dropped in the middle of an Eisenstein-influenced documentary. This is not to say that it appears unmediated: Victor is very aware he's being watched. At one point the crew asks him to sign a paper giving them permission to film him, and he tells them his name is "so long you better have a paper long enough. Wait, I've just started—and I eliminated the middle part"—and Victor's enormous, expanding signature, more powerful without visual representation (how long could it be? what *is* it?), fills the off-screen imaginary. Victor's theatricality disrupts the binary of authenticity and mediation, just as Victor himself quickly dispenses with the puritanical homophobia of "Over the Cliff." He might well stand in for what is productive about theatrical performance in the wake of the apparatus: the homeless performer, mobile, unpredictable, polymorphously perverse, sneaks in where he doesn't belong and changes things. Not presence, but nimbleness; not authenticity, but mutability.

One of Greaves's most powerful techniques in *Symbiopsychotaxiplasm Take One* is repetition: the repetition of the written dialogue, the repetitive structure of the shoot, the repeated return to the crew meetings. The revolutionary potential of repetition as a subversion of standard thinking about time is perhaps what interested Greaves about Aurobindo's mysticism; it is also a feature of Strasberg's ideas about performance. In both his writings and his lectures at the Actors Studio, Strasberg insists (repeatedly) that the problem of acting is the problem of repetition: not doing a scene well, but doing it well over and over again. The problem, but also the opportunity: without that problem of repetition there would be no Method acting to help mitigate it, and no *Symbiopsychotaxiplasm*. Repetition in Greaves's film recalls the messianic temporality of revolutionary change imagined by Walter Benjamin: throughout *Symbiopsychotaxiplasm Take One*, there is always the sense that with the next pair of actors, in the next take, everything will be different, the "dialogue will *explode*," change will occur.[50] Greaves's film as a whole has this quality of messianic readiness, as the crew, too, remains on the cusp of revolution. Victor is ready as well: when the crew at last bids him goodbye, he says, "I never like to say goodbye, I like to say 'so long.'" A few seconds later, he amends it: "Ciao! I never say goodbye, I like to say 'ciao.'" As he and the crew walk off together, a dull static roar rises as the camera pans over the trees, and then we return to a familiar scene: Greaves talking to two actors, two different actors. At the end of the credits, the new actress, Audrey Henningham, who is black, claps, to sync the sound; the same audio whine we heard in the beginning rises, and the screen closes in on her face with the title card "Coming Soon: *Symbiopsychotaxiplasm Take Two*." Next time it might be different.

## NOTES

### Introduction

1. Steven Spielberg, Barack Obama, and Tracy Morgan, "President Obama Plays Daniel Day Lewis in White House Skit-Video," *The Guardian* video, April 28, 2013, http://www.theguardian.com/world/video/2013/apr/28/president-obama -plays-daniel-day-lewis-video.

2. The provenance of the video is unknown; in accordance with tradition, the conceit is that the video, like all of the evening's comedy, comes directly from the president himself, although of course it, like the president's speech, was written by staff members and ghostwriters.

3. Sharon Marie Carnicke, *Stanislavsky in Focus: An Acting Master for the Twenty-First Century* (London: Routledge, 2008), 4.

4. The video could also be read as a contemporary version of Aesop's fable "Washing the Ethiop White," which took on a life of its own in the iconography of American racism, including blackface minstrelsy.

5. Quoted in Cullen Dirner, "Gibbs: Crisis Needs Action, Not 'Method Acting,'" *ABC News*, http://abcnews.go.com/blogs/politics/2010/06/gibbs-crisis-needs-action -not-method-acting/ (accessed June 18, 2013).

6. Gay Gibson Cima, *Performing Women* (Ithaca, N.Y.: Cornell University Press, 1993), 1.

7. David Krasner documents the ire directed at Strasberg since the midcentury in the introduction to his edited volume *Method Acting Reconsidered*, which is titled "I Hate Strasberg." David Krasner, *Method Acting Reconsidered: Past, Present, Future* (New York: St. Martin's Press, 2000).

8. Krasner, "I Hate Strasberg," 7.

9. Sue-Ellen Case, *Feminism and Theatre* (New York: Routledge, 1988), 123.

10. J. Ellen Gainor, "Rethinking Feminism, Stanislavsky, and Performance," *Theatre Topics* 12, no. 2 (2002): 167–69. See also Bruce McConachie, *American Theater in the Culture of the Cold War: Producing and Contesting Containment, 1947–1962* (Iowa City: University of Iowa Press, 2003), 89.

11. Richard Schechner, *Performance Theory* (New York: Routledge, 2003), 69–70. First published as *Essays on Performance Theory* in 1977.

12. I thus take up Carnicke's claim that "while Stanislavsky's ideas touched off something very deep in the American psyche, his adopted culture also transformed them." Carnicke, *Stanislavsky in Focus*, 6.

13. Eve Kosofsky Sedgwick, "Paranoid Reading and Reparative Reading, or, You're So Paranoid, You Probably Think This Essay Is about You," in *Touching Feeling: Affect, Pedagogy, Performativity* (Durham, N.C.: Duke University Press, 2003).

14. Carnicke, *Stanislavsky in Focus*, 25–26.

15. Ibid., 107; see William B. Worthen, "Stanislavsky and the Ethos of the Actor," *Theatre Journal* 35 no. 1 (1983): 32–40.

16. Quoted in Carnicke, *Stanislavsky in Focus*, 109. Carnicke uncovers a deep connection between Stanislavsky's interest in Tolstoy and his developing theories of acting.

17. Ibid., 112–113.

18. Robert Gordon, *The Purpose of Playing: Modern Acting Theories in Perspective* (Ann Arbor: University of Michigan Press, 2006), 20–25; Joseph Roach, *The Player's Passion: Studies in the Science of Acting* (Cranbury, N.J.: Associated University Presses, 1985), 210.

19. Both the terms and goals of Stanislavsky's work correspond in important ways to the innovations of realism and naturalism, although it is important to remember that transformations in representational codes of acting had been described as "realistic" for at least a century prior to the development of realism as a literary genre. Carnicke argues that this was an ironic association, given that Stanislavsky's own practices "moved beyond Realism, and established a System which he did not associate with any particular artistic style" (*Stanislavsky in Focus*, 28). Carnicke argues that Nemirovich-Danchenko was the "true champion of Realism" (ibid., 30).

20. See Gordon, *The Purpose of Playing*, 39, and Carnicke, *Stanislavsky in Focus*, 72.

21. Carnicke, *Stanislavsky in Focus*, 18.

22. His publication in 1923 in *Theatre Arts Magazine* was the first published article on the System. Ibid., 13–22, 36–38. See also Rhonda Blair, introduction to Richard Boleslavsky, *Acting: The First Six Lessons: Documents from the American Laboratory Theater* (London: Routledge, 2010).

23. See Harold Clurman, *The Fervent Years: The Group Theatre and the Thirties* (1975; New York: Da Capo Press, 1983), especially parts 2, 3, and 4.

24. For Clurman's account of the visit, which differs from the story usually told, see ibid., 137–38. Whereas typical accounts make it seem like Adler went to Paris in order to visit Stanislavsky, Clurman's book explains that the two of them went to Paris after a visit in Moscow and heard by chance, through Jacques Copeau, that Stanislavsky was there.

25. Rose Whyman, *The Stanislavsky System of Acting: Legacy and Influence in Modern Performance* (New York: Cambridge University Press, 2008), 244–48. See also Carnicke, *Stanislavsky in Focus*, 31.

26. A clearer picture of his work has emerged from recent scholarship, such as Jean Benedetti's new translations of his writing. See Constantin Stanislavski, *An Actor's Work*, trans. Jean Benedetti (New York: Routledge, 2008).

27. Peter B. Flint, "Stella Adler, 91, Actress and Teacher of the Method," *New York Times*, December 22, 1992. See Stella Adler, *The Art of Acting* (New York: Applause Books, 2000).

28. See Sanford Meisner and Dennis Longwell, *Sanford Meisner on Acting* (New York: Vintage, 1987).

29. UCD 339A, Actors Studio, Wisconsin Theater and Film / Wisconsin Historical Society Archives. Audio recordings. These audio recordings were edited by Robert H. Hethmon and published as *Strasberg at The Actors Studio: Tape-Recorded Sessions* (New York: Theater Communications Group, 1965).

30. See Hans-Thies Lehmann, *Postdramatic Theatre*, trans. Karen Jürs-Munby (London: Routledge, 2006).

31. Stanislavsky developed his system not only because the plays of Chekhov were different but because they were *better* than the Russian plays that preceded them. With the exception of Ostrovsky, Stanislavsky thought that all previous drama was "mediocre." In *An Actor's Work*, Stanislavsky describes the relationship thus: "To bring the mediocre drama written between 1860 and 1890 (if you discount Ostrovski) to life actors could make do with the knowledge they obtained from their own circle and the strata of society attached to it. But when Chekhov wrote *The Seagull*, which is shot through with the atmosphere of a new era, earlier material proved inadequate and we had to dig deeper into the life of our society as a whole and humankind" (Stanislavski, *An Actor's Work*, 226). For Stanislavsky's 1908 reflections on the relationship between Chekhov and the development of his system, see Stanislavski, *Stanislavski's Legacy*, trans. Elizabeth Reynolds Hapgood (New York: Routledge, 1999).

32. William Coyle and Harvey G. Damaser, *Six Early American Plays* (New York: Charles E. Merrill, 1968), xv.

33. Clurman, *The Fervent Years*, 25–26.

34. David Kurnick, *Empty Houses: Theatrical Failure and the Novel* (Princeton, N.J.: Princeton University Press, 2012), 194, 198.

35. Rebecca Schneider, *Performing Remains: Art and War in Times of Theatrical Reenactment* (New York: Routledge, 2011), 168.

36. For instance, see ibid., 39.

37. For the list of playwrights used, see Robert H. Hethmon, ed., *Strasberg at the Actors Studio: The Tape-Recorded Sessions* (New York: Viking, 1965), 410–11. See also David Garfield, *A Player's Place: A Story of the Actors Studio* (New York: Macmillan, 1980). Williams appears throughout the book; see especially 74–75, 84–85, 99–100, 102.

38. Tennessee Williams, *Memoirs* (New York: New Directions, 1972), 167.

39. Carnicke, *Stanislavsky in Focus*, 50; Garfield, *A Player's Place*, 58–59.

40. Colin Counsell, *Signs of Performance* (London: Routledge, 1996), 52–70. See also Shelly Frome, *The Actors Studio: A History* (Jefferson, N.C.: McFarland and Co., 2001), 64–66.

41. Cima, *Performing Women*, 19.

42. Ibid.

43. S.v. "method, n.," *OED Online*, Oxford University Press, http://www .oed.com/view/Entry/117560?isAdvanced=false&result=1&rskey=IDrBH4& (accessed June 18, 2013).

44. Jameson continues: "There exists, no doubt, some impersonal instinct, a life-anxiety of what is improperly personalized and anthropomorphized by the term 'self' in the expression self-preservation, which is manifested in the mute terror of birds, for example, in the face of the spread-eagled remains of one of their species nailed upon a barn door; and embodied even more ambiguously by the crowding of humans, full of visceral fascination and pleasurable horror, in front of a human corpse." Fredric Jameson, *Brecht and Method* (London: Verso, 1998), 53.

45. As Eva Badowska writes, Freud "summons up a veritable storm of analogies and metaphors to describe the phenomenon of identification." Eva Badowska, "Genius Loci: The 'Place' of Identification in Psychoanalysis," *Psychoanalytic Review* 95, no. 6 (December 2008): 955.

46. Sigmund Freud, *The Interpretation of Dreams*, trans. Joyce Crick (Oxford: Oxford University Press, 2008), 117.

47. Diana Fuss, *Identification Papers: Readings on Psychoanalysis, Sexuality, and Culture* (New York: Routledge, 1995), 2.

48. The term also allows me to intervene in the second-wave feminist critique of Method acting using some of its own terms. The insights of Elin Diamond, for instance, who argues that the theater of Adrienne Kennedy demonstrates "the radical power of identification to override the constraints of identity," have much to say to an analysis of the workings of Method acting; indeed, the feminist performance artists she reads in the last section of her book (Peggy Shaw, Robbie McCauley, and Deb Margolin), all of whom use personal monologues that mine their memories and past emotions, could be seen as radical deployers of Method acting, as David Krasner asserts in *Method Acting Reconsidered*, which includes an essay by Margolin that corroborates it. Elin Diamond, *Unmaking Mimesis: Essays on Feminism and Theater* (New York: Routledge, 1997), 126. Krasner, "I Hate Strasberg," 12–13; Deb Margolin, "Mining My Own Business: Paths between Text and Self," in Krasner, *Method Acting Reconsidered*.

49. In fact, the confusion of the two terms goes back to the nineteenth-century English translations of Théodule Ribot, the psychologist who inspired Stanislavsky to develop his exercise: Ribot's original essay was titled "La Memoire Affective"—it was translated and included in an English book titled *The Psychology of Emotions*.

50. Sarah Ahmed, "Affective Economies," *Social Text* 23, nos. 3–4 (2005): 119–20.

51. Ibid., 124.

52. Susan Sontag, "Notes on Camp," in *Against Interpretation and Other Essays* (New York: Farrar, Straus and Giroux, 1966), 285.

53. Andrew Ross, "Uses of Camp," in *No Respect: Intellectuals and Popular Culture* (New York: Routledge, 1989), 151.

## "She's Crazy"

1. *The Misfits*, DVD, directed by John Huston (1961; Santa Monica, Calif.: MGM Home Entertainment, 2001).

2. *Making the Misfits*, DVD, directed by Gail Levin (Arlington, Va.: PBS Great Performances, 2002).

3. Cindy Adams, *Lee Strasberg: The Imperfect Genius of the Actors Studio* (Garden City, N.Y.: Doubleday, 1980), 253–70.

4. Ibid., 271–75. See also Barbara Leaming, *Marilyn Monroe* (New York: Random House, 1998), 159–62.

5. Shelly Frome, *The Actors Studio: A History* (Jefferson, N.C.: McFarland and Co., 2001), 123.

6. Leaming writes, "Marilyn's reverence for Strasberg prevented her from seeing what was evident to many others . . . Far from being sincerely concerned with Marilyn's needs, Strasberg had instantly perceived in the great movie star an opportunity for his own salvation" (*Marilyn Monroe*, 169). While this seems harsh, it demonstrates the resentment many both within and outside the Studio felt regarding Strasberg's relationship to Monroe.

7. In *Making the Misfits*, she is described as "a big black raven," "a sinister figure," "a big black widow spider." *Making the Misfits* DVD. Transcription my own.

8. Case, *Feminism and Theatre*, 122.

9. Rosemary Malague, *An Actress Prepares: Women and "the Method"* (New York: Routledge, 2012), 62–71.

10. Malague rigorously documents the sexism in Strasberg's teaching in *An Actress Prepares*. See ibid., 48–71.

11. Bruce McConachie, "Method Acting and the Cold War," *Theatre Survey* 41, no. 1 (May 2000): 53.

12. Malague, *An Actress Prepares*, 48.

13. Diamond, *Unmaking Mimesis*, 4.

14. Ibid., 6.

15. New Republic, "Across the Great Divide," *New Republic*, February 20, 1961. www.newrepublic.com/article/film/across-the-great-divide#. The web edition denotes the authors as "The New Republic," but David Savran quotes Stanley Kauffman as the author, and I have followed Savran's lead. Savran, *Communists, Cowboys, and Queers: The Politics of Masculinity in the Work of Arthur Miller and Tennessee Williams* (Minneapolis: University of Minnesota Press, 1992), 48.

16. Monroe was apparently dissatisfied with the scene; her own comments corroborate Savran's reading that she felt infantilized, her objections not taken seriously. Jacqueline Rose, "A Rumbling of Things Unknown," *London Review of Books* 34, no. 8 (April 26, 2012): 29–34.

17. *The Misfits*.

18. Savran, *Communists, Cowboys, and Queers*, 49.

## Chapter 1

1. For an introduction to *Acting* and to Boleslavsky, see Rhonda Blair, introduction to *Acting: The First Six Lessons: Documents from the American Laboratory Theatre* by Richard Boleslavsky, ed. Rhonda Blair (New York: Routledge, 2010).

2. Richard Boleslavsky, *Acting: The First Six Lessons* (New York: Theatre Arts Books, 1933), 59.

3. Ibid., 60.

4. Ibid., 61.

5. Richard Hornby, *The End of Acting: A Radical View* (New York: Applause Books, 2000), 32. For a particularly pointed view of the relationship between Strasberg's Method and psychoanalysis, see John Elsom, *Cold War Theatre* (New York: Routledge, 1992), 18–20. More recently, there has been further debate about the extent to which Strasberg borrowed from Freud. Fascinatingly, both Hornby's attack and Krasner's defense include a paradoxical acknowledgment and refusal of the relationship. Hornby marshals the theories of Freud and Lacan as evidence against the "rigid, unchanging self" of Method acting, but also derides American acting teachers who treat their students "as if they were mentally ill" (*The End of Acting*, 34). Krasner declares that "while the Method may borrow from Freudian psychology, it is fundamentally not Freudian but Pavlovian," while simultaneously demonstrating the Method's reliance on the self and personal experience, the "inside-out" approach opposed to behaviorism ("I Hate Strasberg," 13).

6. Sherman Ewing, "Wanted: More Stars, Less 'Method,'" in *Theatre Arts on Acting*, ed. Laurence Senelick (1961; New York: Routledge, 2008), 280.

7. Andrew Sarris, *The American Cinema: Directors and Directions, 1929–1968* (1968; New York: Da Capo, 1996), 158. Sarris reports that he wrote this in 1963.

8. Diamond, *Unmaking Mimesis*, 37–38.

9. Diamond very briefly relates Stanislavsky's psychological techniques to a psychoanalytic case history, but does not go into detail. Ibid., 29–30.

10. Kairschner relates Charcot's hypnosis and contemporary medical technologies, like the X-ray, that ordered internal life into visible expressions to Stanislavsky's production practices, reading Stanislavsky's actors as passive and out of control: "Stanislavsky's actors, deeply absorbed, their bodies affectively deadened, were rendered transparent in order that their bodies might vividly convey 'active' and alive psychic material belonging to an expert somatographer" (385). Interestingly, he doesn't mention Ribot. Kairschner, "Coercive Somatographies: X-rays, Hypnosis, and Stanislavsky's Production Plan for *The Seagull*," *Modern Drama* 51, no. 3 (2008): 372.

11. Jonathan Pitches's *Science and the Stanislavsky System of Acting* exhaustively connects Stanislavsky and his descendants to psychology and behavioral science, comparing the Adler/Strasberg split to the split in American psychology between psychoanalysis and behaviorism and demonstrating how Boleslavsky shifted the terms of Stanislavsky's experiments to give them a more psychoanalytic cast. Jonathan Pitches, *Science and the Stanislavsky System of Acting* (London: Routledge, 2006). See chapter 3, "The·System, Psychology and the US."

12. Michel Foucault, *The History of Sexuality, Vol. 1*, trans. Robert Hurley (New York: Vintage, 1990), 15–50.

13. Hornby, *The End of Acting*, 33–34.

14. W. D. King, "'The Shadow of a Mesmerizer': The Female Body on the 'Dark' Stage," *Theatre Journal* 49, no. 2 (May 1997): 192; Diamond, *Unmaking Mimesis*, chapter 1, especially 9–14.

15. Asti Hustvedt, *Medical Muses: Hysteria in Nineteenth-Century Paris* (New York: W. W. Norton, 2011), 78, 81. See also Georges Didi-Huberman, *Invention of Hysteria: Charcot and the Photographic Iconography of the Salpêtrière*, trans. Alisa Hartz (Cambridge, Mass.: MIT Press, 2003), 175–257.

16. Didi-Huberman, *Invention of Hysteria*, 243.

17. Hustvedt, *Medical Muses*, 109, 93, 32.

18. George Makari, *Revolution in Mind: The Creation of Psychoanalysis* (New York: HarperCollins, 2008), 18.

19. Together, Charcot and Ribot founded the Society of Physiological Psychology in 1885. Serge Nicholas, Yannick Gounden, and Zachary Levine, "The Memory of Two Great Mental Calculators: Charcot and Binet's Neglected 1893 Experiments," *American Journal of Psychology* 124, no. 2 (Summer 2011): 235–42. See also Makari, *Revolution in Mind*. Makari gives Ribot pride of place at the beginning of his book and asserts the key importance of his *psychologie nouvelle* (*Revolution in Mind*, 10–14). See also J. W. Baird, "Théodule Armand Ribot," *American Journal of Psychology* 28, no. 2 (April 1917).

20. Eric Bentley, "Who Was Ribot? Or: Did Stanislavsky Know Any Psychology?," *Tulane Drama Review* 7, no. 2 (Winter 1962): 127–29.

21. He read two of his books that year, *Les Maladies de la Memoire (Diseases of Memory)* and *Les Maladies de la Volonté (Diseases of the Will)*, and two more in the following year: *La Logique des Sentiments (The Logic of Sentiment)* and the essay "La Memoire Affective" ("Affective Memory"). Whyman also demonstrates how and why Stanislavsky's interest in Ribot was later suppressed by Soviet authorities, who viewed Ribot's theories as politically suspect. Whyman, *The Stanislavsky System of Acting*, 52–53.

22. Carnicke, *Stanislavsky in Focus*, 132.

23. See Roach, *The Player's Passion*.

24. Makari, *Revolution in Mind*, 12–13, 18.

25. Douglas W. Alden, "Proust and Ribot," *Modern Language Notes* 58, no. 7 (1943): 501–7.

26. Théodule Ribot, *The Psychology of the Emotions*, trans. unknown (London: Walter Scott Ltd., 1897), 154–55.

27. Boleslavsky, *Acting*, 26.

28. Ibid., 54.

29. Ibid., 68.

30. Ibid., 71.

31. Because the publication of *Acting* preceded the first English translation of Stanislavsky, Elizabeth Reynolds Hapgood's *An Actor Prepares* (New York: Theater Arts Books, 1936), by three years, it was the first exposure American theater artists had to the ideas. Although many scholars have argued that Hapgood's translation itself put too much emphasis on Stanislavsky's experiments in internal acting (making Stanislavsky sound too psychological), the difference between the two books is instructive. Both books are narrated in the first person, and both are fictionalized accounts of an actor's training, but *An Actor Prepares* invites the reader into the journey of the actor, whose revelations, though guided by the director Tortsov, are his own, while *Acting* locates knowledge in "I," the unnamed teacher; in *An Actor Prepares*, we see the student's home, watch him rehearse in his bedroom, and follow the evolution of his thinking, whereas in *Acting*, even though as the book unfolds we hear she has built up a successful career as an actress, the Creature remains secondary. That Stanislavsky's student is male, and Boleslavsky's is female, further highlighted the contrast: Boleslavsky's Creature is much more passive, pliable, and submissive, and arguably paved the way for similar power relations between Strasberg and female actresses.

32. See Joel Pfister, *Staging Depth: Eugene O'Neill and the Politics of Psychological Discourse* (Chapel Hill: University of North Carolina Press, 1995). See Krasner, *Method Acting Reconsidered*, 13.

33. Rosemary Malague also documents Strasberg's medical language in *An Actress Prepares*, 48–56.

34. Lola Cohen, ed., *The Lee Strasberg Notes* (New York: Routledge, 2010), 7–42.

35. Lee Strasberg, *A Dream of Passion* (Boston: Little, Brown, 1987), 139.

36. Ibid., 144.

37. Cohen, *The Lee Strasberg Notes*, 26.

38. Ibid., 30.

39. In a 1964 interview with Richard Schechner, Strasberg stresses that affective memory (by which he seems to include not just emotion but all of the actor's

memories used in performance) must be "remembered emotion," attributing this idea to Vakhtangov. Strasberg and Schechner, "Working with Live Material," *Tulane Drama Review* 9, no. 1 (Autumn 1964): 132. Cohen, *The Lee Strasberg Notes*, 27. See also S. Lorraine Hull, *Strasberg's Method as Taught by Lorrie Hull* (Woodbridge, Conn.: Ox Bow, 1985), 38: "Strasberg stressed the term reliving, not just remembering, explaining that the difference is between knowing something and truly recreating it." Carnicke argues that this word may have originally been a mistranslation of the word she translates as "experiencing," *perezhivanie.* See Carnicke, *Stanislavsky in Focus*, 107–12.

40. Strasberg also cites the importance of relaxation as one of Stanislavsky's key discoveries. Lee Strasberg and Richard Schechner, "Working with Live Material," *Tulane Drama Review* 9, no. 1 (Autumn 1964): 119–21.

41. Strasberg, *A Dream of Passion*, 149–51.

42. UCD 339/A62 (2 of 2) UCD Box 26, Actors Studio, "Affective Memory (Anna Stanovich)," April 19, 1966, Wisconsin Theater and Film Collection / Wisconsin Historical Society Archives. Audio recording.

43. Didi-Huberman, *Invention of Hysteria*, 232.

44. Asti Hustvedt, *Medical Muses: Hysteria in Nineteenth-Century Paris* (New York: W. W. Norton, 2011), 74–75.

45. The centrality of repetition for acting technique was, of course, developed and expanded on by Sanford Meisner, who based his own teaching method on the "repetition exercise." Whereas Strasberg saw theatrical repetition as the actor's problem, Meisner's exercise was designed to trigger interaction between the actors on stage.

46. Malague, *An Actress Prepares*, 206.

47. Ruth Leys, *Trauma: A Genealogy* (Chicago: University of Chicago Press, 2000), 87.

48. Leys: "Now a revealing feature of the 1920 debate in this regard was the fear that, in the absence of cognitive insight, the hypnotic reliving of the trauma might he positively harmful to the patient by reinforcing an emotional dependence on the physician that was held to be incompatible with psychical autonomy and self-control." Ibid., 87.

49. Ibid., 8.

50. Ibid., 48.

51. Ibid., 31.

52. Ibid., 32.

## Chapter 2

1. The origin of this theory may be Stanley Kauffmann's controversial 1966 article in the *New York Times*, "Homosexual Drama and Its Disguises," which caused a stir for pointing out that the three most popular playwrights of the time (recognized as Williams, Edward Albee, and William Inge) were homosexuals, and suggesting that they had a misguided view of marriage and women. Kauffman, "Homosexual Drama and Its Disguises," *New York Times*, January 23, 1966.

2. Marc Robinson, *The American Play 1787–2000* (New Haven, Conn.: Yale University Press, 2009), 270–71.

3. Sontag, "Notes on Camp," 291–92.

4. For a description of Williams's experience in analysis, see Michael Paller, *Gentlemen Callers: Tennessee Williams, Homosexuality, and Twentieth-Century Drama* (New York: Palgrave Macmillan, 2005), 122–33.

5. Kubie apparently loved the play and found the portrayal of the doctor sympathetic. Second of all, as his archives reveal, Kubie was vocal about (and somewhat amused by) Williams's public fabrications regarding his treatment. There is no way of knowing what happened in Dr. Kubie's office, but what does seem clear is that Williams found psychoanalysis creatively generative, both as inspiration and as useful antagonist, and he seems to have had some fun inventing horrors, knowing that Kubie could not return the comment. Letter from Max Greenhouse to Lawrence S. Kubie, March 31, 1962, Tennessee Williams folder, Research and Working Papers, 1940–70, Lawrence S. Kubie Archives, Library of Congress, Washington, D.C.

6. Williams, *The Theatre of Tennessee Williams*, 3:349.

7. Ibid., 3:350.

8. Ibid., 3:349–51.

9. Ibid., 3:375.

10. Ibid., 3:360.

11. Sigmund Freud, *Group Psychology and the Analysis of the Ego*, trans. James Strachey, Kindle edition (Kindle Location 553).

12. Strasberg, *Strasberg at the Actors Studio*, 35.

13. Otto Fenichel, "On Acting," *Tulane Drama Review* 4, no. 3 (1960): 152.

14. Ibid., 154.

15. Ibid., 156.

16. Quoted in Janice Siegel, "Tennessee Williams's *Suddenly Last Summer* and Euripedes's *Bacchae*," *International Journal of the Classical Tradition* 11, no. 4 (2005): 569.

17. Even Gore Vidal, who wrote the screenplay, disliked Mankiewicz's choice: "Joe Mankiewicz was generally good until the liberal rendering of the ending, which was a huge error." Quoted in Siegel, "Tennessee Williams's *Suddenly Last Summer*," 568.

18. Kevin Ohi, "Devouring Creation: Cannibalism, Sodomy and the Scene of Analysis in *Suddenly, Last Summer*," *Cinema Journal* 38, no. 3 (1999): 27–49.

19. Williams, *The Theatre of Tennessee Williams*, 3:386.

20. This is Breuer and Freud's famous hypothesis about hysterics. Ibid., 3:374.

21. Lee Edelman, *No Future: Queer Theory and the Death Drive* (Durham, N.C.: Duke University Press, 2004), 26.

22. Williams, *The Theatre of Tennessee Williams*, 3:397–98.

23. Ibid., 3:398–99.

24. Grey's performance itself is unfortunately not on the tape, so it's impossible to say for sure that she was working on Catharine's monologue, but it seems likely, both because it's the most unified and autonomous monologue in the play and because of Strasberg's response to it.

25. UCD 339A/65 (1 of 2), UCD Box 26, Actors Studio, Wisconsin Center for Film and Theater Research, Wisconsin Historical Society Archives. Audio recording. Transcription my own.

26. Ibid.

27. Williams, *The Theatre of Tennessee Williams*, 3:400.

28. Ibid., 3:402.

29. Alan Sinfield, in *Out on Stage*, calls *Suddenly Last Summer* "Williams' most homophobic play." Sinfield, *Out on Stage: Lesbian and Gay Theater in the Twentieth-Century* (Bath, U.K.: Bath Press, 1999), 192.

30. Williams, *The Theatre of Tennessee Williams*, 3:419.

31. Ibid., 3:423.

32. MS Thr 397 (474), Harvard Theatre Collection, Houghton Library, Harvard University.

33. Strasberg, *Strasberg at the Actors Studio*, 76–77.

### State Servant

1. Gordon Rogoff, "Lee Strasberg: Burning Ice," *Tulane Drama Review* 9, no. 2 (Winter 1964): 136–37, 154, 139, 154. The reference, in the final line, to the Cole Porter song "My Heart Belongs to Daddy" is almost certainly also a reference to Marilyn Monroe, who sang the song in her 1960 film *Let's Make Love*. The characterization of Strasberg as Daddy was recently revived by Rosemary Malague, as I mentioned in part 1, via Ellen Donkin and Susan Clement's feminist directing critique *Upstaging Big Daddy: Directing Theater as if Gender and Race Matter* (Ann Arbor: University of Michigan Press, 1993).

2. See McConachie, "Method Acting and the Cold War"; Marianne Conroy, "Acting Out: Method Acting, the National Culture, and the Middlebrow Disposition in Cold War America," *Criticism* 35, no. 2 (Spring 1993): 239–64.

3. Louis Scheeder, "Strasberg's Method and the Ascendency of American Acting," in *Training of the American Actor*, ed. Arthur Bartow (New York: Theater Communications Group, 2006), 3.

4. Eric Bentley, ed., *Thirty Years of Treason* (New York: Viking, 1971), 492–93.

5. Ibid., 428, 658–59.

6. Litvak, *The Un-Americans*, 20.

7. Ibid., 111.

8. Ibid., 119.

9. There is nothing subtle about this portrayal: a recent photo spread in the *New York Daily News* included a photo of Paula Strasberg and Monroe with a caption that described the photo as giving "the feeling of this Svengali, this woman that was really in total control of Marilyn." See "Marilyn Monroe in 1962: Never-Before-Seen Shots of the American Sex Symbol," *New York Daily News*, May 31, 2012, http://www.nydailynews.com/entertainment/marilyn-monroe-1962-never -before-seen-shots-american-sex-symbol-gallery-1.1086862?pmSlide=7.

10. Eric Bentley, *Thirty Years of Treason*, 487, 489.

11. Folder F150, The Elia Kazan Collection, Wesleyan Cinema Archive, Wesleyan University, Middletown, Conn.

12. Indeed, the call to unmask Strasbergian "mind control" remains visible in castigations of Method acting today. See, for example, Malague, "Emotional Control: Strasberg as Big Daddy of the Method," in *An Actress Prepares*.

13. Litvak, *The Un-Americans*, 15.

### Chapter 3

1. James Baldwin, *Tell Me How Long the Train's Been Gone* (New York: Dell, 1968), 221.

2. Ibid., 223.

3. Ibid., 228–30.

4. James Campbell, *Talking at the Gates* (Berkeley: University of California Press, 1991), 126–27.

5. The Unit presented a dramatic version of Mailer's novel *The Deer Park*, which Baldwin attended. See Baldwin, "The Black Boy Looks at the White Boy," in *Nobody Knows My Name* (New York: Dell, 1961), 171–90. See also Garfield, *A Player's Place*.

6. Baldwin, "Notes for Blues," in *Blues for Mister Charlie* (1964; repr., New York: First Vintage International Edition, 1995), xiii–xv.

7. See Mario Puzo's painful review in the *New York Times*: "This is a simple-minded, one-dimensional novel with mostly cardboard characters, a polemical rather than narrative tone, weak invention and poor selection of incident." Puzo, "Tell Me How Long the Train's Been Gone," *New York Times*, June 23, 1968.

8. Campbell, *Talking at the Gates*, 192–93.

9. Quoted in Campbell, *Talking at the Gates*, 196. See also Garfield, *A Player's Place*, 230–33.

10. See James Baldwin, "Sermons and Blues," *New York Times*, March 29, 1959; LeRoi Jones, "Brief Reflections on Two Hotshots," in *Home: Social Essays* (1963; repr., New York: Akashic Books, 2009). Quoted in Campbell, *Talking at the Gates*, 174.

11. Baldwin, "Theater: The Negro In and Out," in *The Cross of Redemption: Uncollected Writings*, ed. Randall Kenan (New York: Vintage, 2010), 20.

12. Ibid.

13. Campbell, *Talking at the Gates*, 192.

14. After all, LeRoi Jones / Amiri Baraka's radical one-act *The Dutchman* premiered at the downtown Cherry Lane Theater in the same year; Baldwin had other options for production.

15. Quoted in Campbell, *Talking at the Gates*, 195.

16. See, for instance, Gordon, *The Purpose of Playing*, 73.

17. Graham Richards, *"Race," Racism and Psychology* (London: Routledge, 1997), 77–113.

18. Ibid., 133–64.

19. Ibid., 164.

20. Nancy Schnog, "On Inventing the Psychological," in *Inventing the Psychological: Towards a Cultural History of Emotional Life in America*, ed. Nancy Schnog and Joel Pfister (New Haven, Conn.: Yale University Press, 1997), 5.

21. Ellen Herman, *The Romance of American Psychology* (Berkeley: University of California Press, 1995), 199–204, 204.

22. Baldwin, "Notes for Blues," xiv.

23. Meredith M. Malburne, "No Blues for Mister Henry: Locating Richard's Revolution," in *Reading Contemporary African American Drama: Fragments of History, Fragments of Self*, ed. Trudier Harris (New York: Peter Lang, 2007), 39. Malburne's article critiques this common understanding of Richard, arguing that he "creates an opening—however small—for the possibility of revolution" (40).

24. Baldwin, *Blues for Mister Charlie*, 17.

25. Malburne, "No Blues for Mister Henry," 40.

26. Baldwin, *Blues for Mister Charlie*, 2.

27. See Cindy Patton, *Cinematic Identity: Anatomy of a Problem Film* (Minneapolis: University of Minnesota Press, 2007), 88.

28. Baldwin, *Blues for Mister Charlie*, 3.

29. Ibid., 81, 45.

30. Ibid., 97.

31. Ibid., 103–5.

32. Ibid., 115.

33. David Wiles launches a similar critique of the Method to the one I have explored in *Blues for Mister Charlie*. Discussing his personal experience as an African American Method actor, Wiles argues that the key problem with the Method is that it leaves out the audience. This is a serious problem because it denies the primary reality of the theater: "Race and all the other inescapable socio/political facts shatter the fourth wall by asserting their presence into whatever theatrical 'reality' is being presented" (173). Wiles argues that the actor who is attuned to these "inescapable socio/political facts" and how they affect how his or her performance is received will in fact be a better Method actor, insofar as he or she will be more truthful in his or her given circumstances. Wiles also suggests that the convention of the fourth wall, and the exclusion of the audience that it represents, is itself culturally exclusionary. He cites his experience as an audience member at August Wilson's *Fences*: to the surprise and chagrin of other audience members, many African American audience members talked through the performance, breaking the "mainstream" (i.e., white) convention of audience silence, and behaving as they would in church. It was a shame, Wiles writes, that the actors, whether by habit or training, did not acknowledge what was actually happening in the theater. As I have shown, *Blues for Mister Charlie* makes many of the same points dramatically that Wiles makes in his essay. See Wiles, "Burdens of Representation," in *Method Acting Reconsidered*, 169–78.

34. Garfield, *A Player's Place*, 242; Campbell, *Talking at the Gates*, 199.

35. Philip Roth, "Channel X: Two Plays on the Race Conflict," *New York Review of Books*, May 28, 1964.

36. Baldwin, *Blues for Mister Charlie*, 94.

37. Although my evidence is anecdotal, it is interesting to note, in this vein, that this monologue is a popular audience piece for actresses: as one friend explained to me, "It's got everything—every emotional level." The monologue is included in the Routledge collection *The Modern Monologue: Women* (New York: Routledge, 1993).

38. Baldwin, *Tell Me How Long the Train's Been Gone*, 264.

39. James Baldwin, *Another Country* (New York: Vintage, 1962), 195. Kurnick emphasizes the placement of Stanislavsky between Henry James's *The Wings of the Dove* and Richard Wright's *Native Son*, which he reads as "suggesting the theater's mediating role between the supposed quintessentially 'psychological' ground of the former and the clearly 'political' scope of the latter." Kurnick, *Empty Houses*, 216.

40. Stanislavsky, *An Actor Prepares*, 2.

41. Ibid., 5.

42. Ibid., 8–9.

43. Ibid., 10.

44. Ibid., 26.

45. Patton, *Cinematic Identity*, 3.

## Chapter 4

1. This question also reflects what David Savran calls "the almost incessant cross-fertilization" of realism and expressionism "since the Renaissance." Savran, *Communists, Cowboys, and Queers*, 30.

2. Edmund White, *Genet: A Biography* (London: Vintage Books, 1993), 402.

3. Maya Angelou, "James Baldwin: His Voice Remembered; A Brother's Love," *New York Times*, December 20, 1987, section 7, http://www.nytimes.com/books /98/03/29/specials/baldwin-angelou.html?_r=1.

4. *Jean Genet's The Blacks: A Panel Discussion*. Directed by James Briggs Murray. Participants: Amiri Baraka, Roscoe Lee Browne, Ed Bullins, Vinnie Burrows, Michael Dinwiddie, Gene Frankel, Arthur French, Ty Jones, and Judith Malina. Schomburg Center for Research in Black Culture, New York Public Library, New York, February 3, 2003.

5. See Amiri Baraka, "Jimmy!," in *The LeRoi Jones / Amiri Baraka Reader*, ed. William J. Harris (1987; repr., New York: Thunder's Mouth, 1991), 454. For an account of the critical reception of *The Blacks*, see John Warrick, "The Blacks and Its Impact on African American Theater," in *Jean Genet: Performance and Politics*, ed. Clare Finburgh, Carl Lavery, and Maria Shevtsova (London: Palgrave Macmillan, 2006).

6. Genet's famous preface states: "This play, written, I repeat, by a white man, is intended for a white audience, but if, which is unlikely, it is ever performed for a black audience, then a white person, male or female, should be invited every evening . . . But what if no white person accepted? Then let white masks be distributed to the black spectators as they enter the theater. And if the blacks refuse these masks, then let a dummy be used." *The Blacks: A Clown Show*, trans. Bernard Frechtman (New York: Grove, 1966).

7. Una Chaudhuri, *No Man's Stage* (Ann Arbor, Mich.: UMI Research Press, 1986).

8. Peter Brook in Brook et al., "Marat/Sade Forum," *Tulane Drama Review* 10, no. 4 (Summer 1966): 228. Recorded January 28, 1966, Saint Mark's Playhouse, New York.

9. In the original French, his name is Ville St. Nazaire; both refer to coastal industrial cities with large black populations—and although the play seems to take place in postcolonial Africa, the name "Ville St. Nazaire" connects the character directly to the immigrant situation in France.

10. Chaudhuri, *No Man's Stage*, 85.

11. Norman Mailer, "Theatre: The Blacks," *Village Voice*, May 11, 1961, 9.

12. Lorraine Hansberry, "Genet, Mailer, and the New Paternalism," *Village Voice*, June 1, 1961, 10.

13. Ibid., 14, 15.

14. In her understanding of the antihumanist vision of *The Blacks*, Hansberry's rejection of the play seems more on point than the laudatory acceptance of Howard Taubman, who, in the first of his two glowing *New York Times* reviews, concluded that "as an exploration of the heart of the Negro, [the play] moves from anger to aspiration."

15. Genet, *The Blacks*, 12.

16. Ibid., 44–45.

17. Ibid., 46.

18. Ibid., 76.

19. See my second chapter.

20. Genet joined Allen Ginsberg and protested at the 1968 Democratic Convention in Chicago; he toured the United States with the Black Panthers, spoke for Bobby Seale at Yale in 1970, and wrote the introduction to George Jackson's prison memoir *Soledad Brother*; he later joined the Palestinian resistance, chronicling his experience in his last prose work, *Prisoner of Love*. See White, *Genet*.

21. Jean Genet, "Interview with Michèle Manceaux," in *The Declared Enemy: Texts and Interviews*, ed. Albert Dichy, trans. Jeff Fort (Stanford, Calif.: Stanford University Press, 2004), 48.

22. "The temptation to 'go over' goes with the unease at having just one simple certainty—a certainty that's bound *ipso facto* to be uncertain. Getting to know the other, who's supposed to be wicked because he's the enemy, makes possible not only battle itself but also close bodily contact between the combatants and between their beliefs. So each doctrine is sometimes the shadow and sometimes the equivalent of the other, sometimes the subject and sometimes the object of new day-dreams and thoughts so complex they can't be disentangled." Genet, *Prisoner of Love*, trans. Barbara Bray (New York: New York Review Books, 2003), 70.

23. Ibid., 302.

24. Ibid., 173.

25. Allan Francovich, "Genet's Theatre of Possession," *The Drama Review: TDR* 14, no. 1 (1969): 30.

26. Herbert Blau, "Fervently Impossible: The Group Idea and Its Legacy," in *The Dubious Spectacle: Extremities of Theater 1976–2000* (Minneapolis: University of Minnesota Press, 2002), 217. See also Richard Schechner, *The End of Humanism: Writings on Performance* (New York: Performing Arts Journal Publications, 1982), 96.

27. Richard Schechner, "Twilight of the Gods," *Tulane Drama Review* 9, no. 2 (Winter 1964): 15–17.

28. Rogoff, "Lee Strasberg: Burning Ice," 138.

29. Lee Strasberg, Gordon Rogoff, and Paul Gray, "Strasberg vs. TDR," *Tulane Drama Review* 11, no. 1 (Autumn 1966): 234–42.

30. Joseph Roach, *Cities of the Dead: Circum-Atlantic Performance* (New York: Columbia University Press, 1996).

31. Allan Francovich, "Genet's Theatre of Possession," *The Drama Review: TDR* 14, no. 1 (1969): 30.

32. Samuel Weber, *Theatricality as Medium* (New York: Fordham University Press, 2004), 7.

33. Roach, *Cities of the Dead*, 76.

34. Ibid., 78.

## Chapter 5

1. Schechner, *Performance Theory*, 72.

2. For instance, John Cassavetes's first feature film, *Shadows*, came directly out of his Method-based acting workshop. See Ray Carney, *Cassavetes on Cassavetes* (New York: Faber and Faber, 2001), 65.

3. I am indebted to Martin Harries for his insight into the specificities of the midcentury relationship between theater and film.

4. Cassavetes's *Shadows* (1958), which came out of his Method-based acting workshop, belongs in this category, as do Martin Scorsese's early films.

5. Scott MacDonald, *Screen Writings: Scripts and Texts by Independent Filmmakers* (Berkeley: University of California Press, 1995), 31.

6. In a provocative, if too brief, recent article called "A Dangerous Method: The Art of Authenticity as a Social Imperative," Jon Leon Torn (the child of Geraldine Page and Rip Torn, two of the most important theater actors of the Actors Studio) discusses the postmodern challenges to Method acting's claims to authenticity and the Method's persistence in film acting: "Modernist foundational authenticity does not melt away under the postmodern challenge, it becomes weird, baroque, overdetermined in its acknowledgement of its constructed nature as well as even more stubbornly insistent on the need for authenticity, the authenticity of authenticity if you will, authenticity to the second power." Jon Leon Torn, "A Dangerous Method: The Art of Authenticity as a Social Imperative," *Liminalities: A Journal of Performance Studies* 7, no. 4 (December 2011): 5.

7. William Inge, *Where's Daddy?* (New York: Dramatists Play Service, 1964), 27–28.

8. Ibid., 28–29.

9. Aamir R. Mufti, "The Aura of Authenticity," *Social Text* 64 (Autumn 2000): 89.

10. Marshall Berman, *The Politics of Authenticity: Radical Individualism and the Emergence of Modern Society* (London: Verso, 2009), 311.

11. Martin Jay, "Taking On the Stigma of Inauthenticity: Adorno's Critique of Genuineness," *New German Critique*, no. 97 (Winter 2006): 16.

12. David Krasner, "I Hate Strasberg," in *Method Acting Reconsidered*, ed. David Krasner (New York: Palgrave Macmillan, 2000), 26.

13. Maurice Zolotow, "The Stars Rise Here," *Saturday Evening Post* (May 18, 1957), 84.

14. Theodor Adorno, *The Jargon of Authenticity*, trans. Knut Tarnowski and Frederic Will (Evanston, Ill.: Northwestern University Press, 1973), 14–22.

15. Ibid., 29.

16. Ibid., 14.

17. Jay, "Taking On the Stigma of Inauthenticity," 19.

18. Martin Harries, "Walter Benjamin on Theater and Crisis" (presentation, American Comparative Literature Association, Brown University, Providence, Rhode Island, March 30–April 1, 2012).

19. See Martin Harries, "Theater and Media before New Media: Beckett's Film and Play," Theater 42, no. 2 (2012): 7–25. Philip Auslander deals extensively with the connection between early television and drama and the issue of "immediacy" in his influential first chapter in *Liveness: Performance in a Mediatized Culture*, which he also explores using Benjamin. See Auslander, *Liveness: Performance in a Mediatized Culture* (New York: Routledge, 1999), 1–72.

20. Inge, *Where's Daddy?*, 8.

21. Ibid., 13.

22. Signed letter from actors to Kazan, unmarked folder, Actors Studio box, Elia Kazan Collection, Wesleyan Cinema Archives, Wesleyan University, Middletown, Conn.

23. Describing her daughter in the second act, Teena's mother waxes poetic: "Now she's like one of those little turtles I saw in that Disney film, trying to make its way to the sea, without being snatched by great birds and devoured" (Inge, *Where's Daddy?*, 60). In *Suddenly Last Summer*, the newborn sea turtles of the Encantadas, devoured by birds as they rush to safety in the sea, is the central image of the play-world: first recounted by Mrs. Venable as an image of her son's search for meaning, then resignified as an image of her son's death. See Tennessee Williams, *The Theatre of Tennessee Williams, vol. 3* (New York: New Directions, 1971).

24. See Robert H. Hethmon, *Strasberg at the Actors Studio: Tape-Recorded Sessions* (New York: Theatre Communications Group, 1965), 23. Lola Cohen's recent edition of *The Lee Strasberg Notes* includes a section of excerpts from these scene critiques (Cohen, *The Lee Strasberg Notes*, 50–70). See also Kazan, *Elia Kazan: A Life* (New York: Alfred A. Knopf, 1988), 439–40. For Strasberg's assertion that the words of the play are secondary to their emotional content, see Foster Hirsch, *A Method to Their Madness: A History of the Actors Studio* (New York: Da Capo Press, 1984), 227. For a brief discussion of this ambivalence related to the on-again, off-again Playwrights Unit, see Hirsch, *A Method to Their Madness*, 227–29.

25. Elia Kazan, unmarked folder, Actors Studio box, Elia Kazan Collection, Wesleyan Cinema Archives, Wesleyan University, Middletown, Conn.

26. Constantin Stanislavsky, *Creating a Role*, trans. Elizabeth Reynolds Hapgood (New York: Routledge, 1961), 11.

27. If Kazan's Actor still sounds like the self-identical, self-present subject, the decisive subject of existentialism, for instance, it is worth remembering that it comes out of a strangely depersonalized anecdote. Marlon Brando is not the subject of this Acting, he is only himself a *medium* for it: he "would know what I was talking about."

28. Walter Benjamin, "The Work of Art in the Age of Its Technological Reproducibility," in *The Work of Art in the Age of Its Technological Reproducibility and Other Writings on Media* (Cambridge, Mass.: Harvard University Press, 2008).

29. *Symbiopsychotaxiplasm Take One*, DVD, directed by William Greaves (1968; New York: Criterion Collection, 2006). All transcriptions are my own.

30. *Symbiopsychotaxiplasm Take One*, like Greaves's career as a whole, reveals a heretofore-obscured relationship between Method acting and documentary, which John Grierson defined as "the creative treatment of actuality." In the famous 1963 argument between Jean Rouch, the inventor of the term "cinema verité," and Richard Leacock, who preferred "direct cinema," both filmmakers insisted that their techniques led to "the reality of life" and "the truth in people": Rouch "attempted to unmask truth through a process of deliberately encouraged self-revelation," while "Leacock tried to expose this reality through capturing unguarded moments of self-revelation in the movement of actual life." The cinema verité / direct cinema debate made clear that by the 1960s, the blurry line between documentary and fiction had become a salient problematic of the form.

These debates around documentary are another crucial piece of context for the debates surrounding Method acting, especially after the 1960s. Jack C. Ellis and Betsy A. McLane, *A New History of Documentary Film* (New York: Continuum, 2005), ix, 217, 221–24.

31. *Symbiopsychotaxiplasm Take One.*

32. Scott Macdonald, *A Critical Cinema 3: Interviews with Independent Film-makers* (Berkeley: University of California Press, 1998), 57.

33. Abigail Cheever, *Real Phonies: Cultures of Authenticity in Post–World War II America* (Athens: University of Georgia Press, 2010), 5.

34. In the second installment, which Greaves made in 2003 but in which he included some of the original 1968 footage, Bob Rosen challenges this idea:

CREW MEMBER: In one thing, you're talking about an irreducible truth, and in another instance, you might be talking about some sort of fantasy—whereby—

ROSEN: What's an irreducible truth?

CREW MEMBER: You're cutting my balls, or whatever.

ROSEN: Why? Do people really have to say that? . . . Why is it an irreducible truth?

*Symbiopsychotaxiplasm Take 2 1/2*, DVD, directed by William Greaves (2003; New York: Criterion Collection, 2006).

35. Herbert Marcuse, *Eros and Civilization: A Philosophical Inquiry into Freud* (Boston: Beacon Press, 1955), 45.

36. *Symbiopsychotaxiplasm Take One.*

37. Adam Knee and Charles Musser, "William Greaves, Documentary Film-making, and the African-American Experience," *Film Quarterly* 45, no. 3 (Spring 1992): 20.

38. William Greaves, "Production Notes," *Symbiopsychotaxiplasm*, Criterion Collection DVD booklet, 2006.

39. Moreno's psychodrama cannot help but stand out given the title of this book: although it does not explicitly appear in the 1968 version, it does in the 2003 sequel, *Symbiopsychotaxiplasm Take 2½*, the first half hour of which was composed entirely of footage from the original 1968 shoot, which reveals that Greaves used Moreno's psychodrama as an improvisatory exercise for the actors to add depth to their characterizations and "remove their blocks." Although Moreno, early on in his career, insisted that his therapeutic technique had nothing to do with Stanislavsky (and was indeed opposed to Stanislavsky), Greaves uses it as an acting exercise that would fit seamlessly into the work of the Actors Studio (where removing actors' blocks was a major concern). See J. L. Moreno, *Psychodrama (First Volume)* (Boston: Beacon House, 1946).

40. As Declan Donnellan puts it in the introduction to Jean Benedetti's new translation of Stanislavsky, "A main theme of [Stanislavksy's] early work does seem to be an escape from 'superficial' theater into something more 'true.' This becomes counterbalanced by the understanding that in fact theatre needs both of these extremities to have any life . . . Like many great artists, Stanislavski navigates between these eternal poles, profane and sacred, rough and holy, earth and

clouds, showbiz and sacrament." See Donnelan, introduction to *An Actor's Work* by Konstantin Stanislavski, trans. and ed. Jean Benedetti (New York: Routledge, 2008), xi.

41. Greaves, "Production Notes."

42. "We return to a status of world in the mind, yet mind in the world. We solve it by symbiotaxis. The World is in the mind socially taken as action (symbiotaxis). The symbiotaxium constructs the world—knowledge—i.e., it 'is' that world. The world (knowledge) includes mind (mind as psychological technique)." Arthur Bentley, *Inquiry into Inquiries: Essays in Social Theory* (Boston: Beacon Press, 1954), 25.

43. Sedgwick, *Touching Feeling*, 9–13.

44. Greaves, "Production Notes."

45. *Symbiopsychotaxiplasm Take One.*

46. Macdonald, *A Critical Cinema*, 51.

47. See Litvak, *The Un-Americans*, chapter 1.

48. Ibid., 20.

49. *Symbiopsychotaxiplasm Take One.*

50. See Walter Benjamin, "Theses on the Philosophy of History," in *Illuminations*, trans. Henry Zohn (New York: Schocken, 1968), 253–64.

# BIBLIOGRAPHY

Actors Studio, UCD 339, Wisconsin Theater and Film Collection / Wisconsin Historical Society Archives. Audio recordings.

Adams, Cindy. *Lee Strasberg: The Imperfect Genius of the Actors Studio.* Garden City, N.Y.: Doubleday, 1980.

Adler, Stella. *The Art of Acting.* New York: Applause Books, 2000.

Adorno, Theodor. *The Jargon of Authenticity.* Translated by Knut Tarnowski and Frederic Will. Evanston, Ill.: Northwestern University Press, 1973.

Ahmed, Sarah. "Affective Economies." *Social Text* 23, nos. 3–4 (2005): 117–39.

Alden, Douglas W. "Proust and Ribot." *Modern Language Notes* 58, no. 7 (1943): 501–7.

Angelou, Maya. "James Baldwin: His Voice Remembered; A Brother's Love." *New York Times*, December 20, 1987. www.nytimes.com/books/98/03/29/specials /baldwin-angelou.html?_r=1.

Archer, William. Introduction to *Dramatic Essays.* Edited by William Archer and Robert W. Lowe. London: Walter Scott Limited, 1896.

Aronson, Arnold. *American Avant-Garde Theatre: A History.* London: Routledge, 2000.

Artaud, Antonin. *The Theater and Its Double.* Translated by Mary Caroline Richards. New York: Grove Press, 1958.

Atkinson, Brooks. "'Garden District': Short Plays by Tennessee Williams Put On in an Off-Broadway House." *New York Times*, January 19, 1958.

Auslander, Philip. "Just Be Your Self: Logocentrism and Difference in Performance Theory." In *Acting (Re)Considered.* Edited by Philip B. Zarrilli. New York: Routledge, 1995.

———. Liveness: Performance in a Mediatized Culture. New York: Routledge, 1999.

*Baby Doll.* Directed by Elia Kazan. DVD. 1956; Burbank, Calif.: Warner Bros. Pictures, 2006.

Badowska, Eva. "Genius Loci: The 'Place' of Identification in Psychoanalysis." *Psychoanalytic Review* 95, no. 6 (December 2008): 947–72.

Baird, J. W. "Théodule Armand Ribot." *American Journal of Psychology* 28, no. 2 (1917): 312–13.

Baldwin, James. *Another Country.* New York: Vintage, 1962.

———. *Blues for Mister Charlie.* New York: Vintage, 1995.

———. *The Cross of Redemption: Uncollected Writings.* Edited by Randall Kenan. New York: Vintage, 2010.

———. *Nobody Knows My Name.* New York: Dell, 1961.

———. "Sermons and Blues." *New York Times*, March 29, 1959. www.nytimes .com/books/98/03/29/specials/baldwin-hughes.html.

———. *Tell Me How Long the Train's Been Gone.* New York: Dell, 1968.

Baraka, Amiri. "Jimmy!" In *The LeRoi Jones / Amiri Baraka Reader.* Edited by William J. Harris. 1987; New York: Thunder's Mouth, 1991.

———. "Tennessee Williams Is Never Apolitical." *Tenn at One Hundred: The Reputation of Tennessee Williams.* Edited by David Kaplan. East Brunswick, N.J.: Hansen, 2011.

Baron, Cynthia, and Sharon Marie Carnicke. *Reframing Screen Performance.* Ann Arbor: University of Michigan Press, 2008.

Beck, Dennis C. "The Paradox of the Method Actor: Rethinking the Stanislavsky Legacy." In *Method Acting Reconsidered,* edited by David Krasner. New York: St. Martin's, 2000.

Benjamin, Walter. *Illuminations.* Translated by Henry Zohn. New York: Schocken, 1968.

———. "The Work of Art in the Age of Its Technological Reproducibility." In *The Work of Art in the Age of Its Technological Reproducibility and Other Writings on Media.* Cambridge, Mass.: Harvard University Press, 2008.

Bentley, Arthur. *Inquiry into Inquiries: Essays in Social Theory.* Boston: Beacon Press, 1954.

Bentley, Eric, ed. *Thirty Years of Treason.* New York: Viking, 1971.

———. "Who Was Ribot? Or: Did Stanislavsky Know Any Psychology?" *Tulane Drama Review* 7, no. 2 (Winter 1962): 127–29.

Berman, Marshall. *The Politics of Authenticity: Radical Individualism and the Emergence of Modern Society.* London: Verso, 2009.

Blair, Rhonda. Introduction to *Acting: The First Six Lessons: Documents from the American Laboratory Theatre* by Richard Boleslavsky. Edited by Rhonda Blair. London: Routledge, 2010.

Blau, Herbert. *The Dubious Spectacle: Extremities of Theater 1976–2000.* Minneapolis: University of Minnesota Press, 2002.

———. *Take Up the Bodies.* Urbana: University of Illinois Press, 1982.

Blum, Richard. *American Film Acting: The Stanislavsky Heritage.* Ann Arbor, Mich.: UMI Research Press, 1984.

Boleslavsky, Richard. *Acting: The First Six Lessons.* New York: Theatre Arts Books, 1933.

Bosworth, Patricia. *Marlon Brando.* New York: Viking, 2001.

Bottoms, Stephen J. "The Efficacy/Effeminacy Braid." *Theater Topics* 13, no. 2 (September 2003): 173–87.

Breuer, Josef, and Sigmund Freud. *Studies on Hysteria.* Translated and edited by James Strachey. New York: Basic Books, 2000.

Brook, Peter, Leslie Fiedler, Geraldine Lust, Roman Podhoretz, Ian Richardson, and Gordon Rogoff. "Marat/Sade Forum." *Tulane Drama Review* 10, no. 4 (Summer 1966): 214–37.

Brooks, Peter. *The Melodramatic Imagination: Balzac, Henry James, Melodrama, and the Mode of Excess.* New Haven, Conn.: Yale University Press, 1995.

Burham, John C. "The New Psychology." In *1915: The Cultural Moment.* Edited by Adele Heller and Lois Rudnick. New Brunswick, N.J.: Rutgers University Press, 1991.

Butler, Judith. *Subjects of Desire.* New York: Columbia University Press, 1987.

Campbell, James. *Talking at the Gates.* Berkeley: University of California Press, 1991.

Carlson, Marvin. *The Haunted Stage.* Ann Arbor: University of Michigan Press, 2001.

Carney, Ray, ed. *Cassavetes on Cassavetes*. London: Faber and Faber, 2001.

Carnicke, Sharon Marie. *Stanislavsky in Focus: An Acting Master for the Twenty-First Century* (London: Routledge, 2008).

Case, Sue-Ellen. *Feminism and Theatre*. New York: Routledge, 1988.

Chaudhuri, Una. *No Man's Stage*. Ann Arbor, Mich.: UMI Research Press, 1986.

Cheever, Abigail. *Real Phonies: Cultures of Authenticity in Post–World War II America*. Athens: University of Georgia Press, 2010.

Cima, Gay Gibson. *Performing Women*. Ithaca, N.Y.: Cornell University Press, 1993.

Clurman, Harold. *The Fervent Years: The Group Theater and the Thirties*. 1975; New York: Da Capo, 1983.

Cohan, Steven. *Masked Men: Masculinity and the Movies in the Fifties*. Bloomington: Indiana University Press, 1997.

Cohen, Lola, ed. *The Lee Strasberg Notes*. New York: Routledge, 2010.

Counsell, Colin. *Signs of Performance*. London: Routledge, 1996.

Coyle, William, and Harvey G. Damaser. *Six Early American Plays*. New York: Charles E. Merrill, 1968.

Crowther, Bosley. "Film Improvised under Cassavetes Opens." *New York Times*, March 22, 1961.

Cvetkovich, Ann. *An Archive of Feelings: Trauma, Sexuality, and Lesbian Public Cultures*. Durham, N.C.: Duke University Press, 2003.

Diamond, Elin. *Unmaking Mimesis: Essays on Feminism and Theater*. New York: Routledge, 1997.

Didi-Huberman, Georges. *Invention of Hysteria: Charcot and the Photographic Iconography of the Salpêtrière*. Translated by Alisa Hartz. Cambridge, Mass.: MIT Press, 2004.

Diggs, Soyika. "Historicizing the Ghostly Sound of a Ghastly Sight: James Baldwin's *Blues for Mister Charlie*." In *Sonic Interventions*, edited by Sylvia Mieszkowski, Joy Smith, and Marijke de Valck. New York: Editions Rodolpi B.V., Amsterdam, 2007.

Dirner, Cullen. "Gibbs: Crisis Needs Action, Not 'Method Acting.'" *ABC News*, abcnews.go.com/blogs/politics/2010/06/gibbs-crisis-needs-action-not-method-acting/ (accessed June 18, 2013).

Display ad for *Blues for Mister Charlie*. *New York Times*, May 28, 1964, 43.

Doherty, Thomas. *Cold War, Cool Medium*. New York: Columbia University Press, 2003.

Dollard, John. *Caste and Class in a Southern Town*. New Haven, Conn.: Yale University Press, 1937.

Donkin, Ellen, and Susan Clement. *Upstaging Big Daddy: Directing Theater as if Gender and Race Matter*. Ann Arbor: University of Michigan Press, 1993.

Donnelan, Declan. Introduction to *An Actor's Work* by Konstantin Stanislavski. Translated and edited by Jean Benedetti. New York: Routledge, 2008.

Easty, Edward Dwight. *On Method Acting*. New York: Ivy, 1981.

Edelman, Lee. *No Future: Queer Theory and the Death Drive*. Durham, N.C.: Duke University Press, 2004.

Ellis, Jack C., and Betsy A. McLane. *A New History of Documentary Film*. New York: Continuum, 2005.

Elsom, John. *Cold War Theatre*. New York: Routledge, 1992.

Esslin, Martin. *The Theater of the Absurd*. New York: Vintage, 1961.

Ewing, Sherman. "Wanted: More Stars, Less 'Method.' " In *Theatre Arts on Acting*, edited by Laurence Senelick. New York: Routledge, 2008.

Fenichel, Otto. "On Acting." *Tulane Drama Review* 4, no. 3 (1960): 148–59.

Fleche, Anne. "When a Door Is a Jar, or Out in the Theatre: Tennessee Williams and Queer Space." *Theatre Journal* 47, no. 2 (1995): 253–67.

Flint, Peter B. "Stella Adler, 91, Actress and Teacher of the Method." *New York Times*, December 22, 1992.

Foucault, Michel. *The History of Sexuality, Vol. 1*. Translated by Robert Hurley. New York: Vintage, 1990.

Freud, Sigmund. *Beyond the Pleasure Principle*. Translated by James Strachey. New York: W. W. Norton, 1961.

———. *Group Psychology and the Analysis of the Ego*. Translated by James Strachey. London: International Psycho-analytical Press, 1922.

———. *The Interpretation of Dreams*. Translated by Joyce Crick. Oxford: Oxford University Press, 2008.

Frome, Shelly. *The Actors Studio: A History*. Jefferson, N.C.: McFarland and Co., 2001.

Fuchs, Elinor. "Clown Shows: Anti-theatricalist Theatricalism in Four Twentieth-Century Plays." In *Against Theater: Creative Destructions on the Modernist Stage*, edited by Alan Ackerman and Martin Pucher. New York: Palgrave Macmillan, 2006.

Fuss, Diana. *Identification Papers: Readings on Psychoanalysis, Sexuality, and Culture*. New York: Routledge, 1995.

Gabler, Neal. *An Empire of Their Own: How the Jews Invented Hollywood*. New York: First Anchor, 1989.

Gainor, J. Ellen. "Rethinking Feminism, Stanislavsky, and Performance." *Theatre Topics* 12, no. 2 (2002): 167–69.

Garfield, David. *A Player's Place: A Story of the Actors Studio*. New York: Macmillan, 1980.

Genet, Jean. *The Blacks*. Translated by Bernard Frechtman. New York: Grove, 1960.

———. "Interview with Michèle Manceaux." In *The Declared Enemy: Texts and Interviews*, edited by Albert Dichy, translated by Jeff Fort. Stanford, Calif.: Stanford University Press, 2004.

———. *Prisoner of Love*. Translated by Barbara Bray. New York: New York Review Books, 2003.

Goldberg, RoseLee. *Performance: Live Art 1909 to the Present*. New York: Harry N. Abrams, 1979.

Gordon, Robert. *The Purpose of Playing: Modern Acting Theories in Perspective*. Ann Arbor: University of Michigan Press, 2006.

Graham-White, Anthony. "Jean Genet and the Psychology of Colonialism." *Comparative Drama* 4, no. 3 (1970).

Greaves, William. "Production Notes." *Symbiopsychotaxiplasm*. Criterion Collection DVD booklet. New York: Criterion Collection, 2006.

———. *Symbiopsychotaxiplasm*. New York: Criterion Collection, 2006.

Gregg, Melissa, and Gregory J. Seigworth, eds. *The Affect Theory Reader*. Durham, N.C.: Duke University Press, 2010.

Hansberry, Lorraine. "Genet, Mailer, and the New Paternalism." *Village Voice,* June 1, 1961.

———. *To Be Young, Gifted, and Black.* New York: Penguin Books, 1969.

Harries, Martin. *Forgetting Lot's Wife.* New York: Fordham University Press, 2004.

———. "Theater and Media before New Media: Beckett's Film and Play." *Theater* 42, no. 2 (2012): 7–25.

Harris, Trudier. *Exorcising Blackness: Historical and Literary Lynching and Burning Rituals.* Bloomington: Indiana University Press, 1984.

Herman, Ellen. *The Romance of American Psychology.* Berkeley: University of California Press, 1995.

Herman, Luc, ed. *Concepts of Realism.* Columbia, S.C.: Camden House, 1996.

Hethmon, Robert, ed. *Strasberg at the Actors Studio: The Tape-Recorded Sessions.* New York: Viking, 1965.

Hirsch, Foster. *Method to Their Madness: A History of the Actors Studio.* New York: Da Capo Press, 1984.

Hischak, Thomas S., and Gerald Martin Bordman. *American Theater: A Chronicle of Comedy and Drama 1869–1914.* New York: Oxford University Press, 1994.

Hornby, Richard. *The End of Acting: A Radical View.* New York: Applause Books, 2000.

Hull, S. Lorraine. *Strasberg's Method as Taught by Lorrie Hull.* Woodbridge, Conn.: Ox Bow, 1985.

Hustvedt, Asti. *Medical Muses: Hysteria in Nineteenth-Century Paris.* New York: W. W. Norton, 2011.

Inge, William. *Where's Daddy?* New York: Dramatists Play Service, 1964.

Jameson, Fredric. *Brecht and Method.* London: Verso, 1998.

Jay, Martin. "Taking On the Stigma of Inauthenticity: Adorno's Critique of Genuineness." *New German Critique,* no. 97 (Winter 2006): 15–30.

*Jean Genet's The Blacks: A Panel Discussion.* Directed by James Briggs Murray. Participants: Amiri Baraka, Roscoe Lee Browne, Ed Bullins, Vinnie Burrows, Michael Dinwiddie, Gene Frankel, Arthur French, Ty Jones, and Judith Malina. Schomburg Center for Research in Black Culture, New York Public Library, New York, February 3, 2003.

Jones, LeRoi. "Brief Reflections on Two Hotshots." In *Home: Social Essays.* New York: Akashic Books, 2009.

Kairschner, Shawn. "Coercive Somatographies: X-rays, Hypnosis, and Stanislavsky's Production Plan for *The Seagull.*" *Modern Drama* 51, no. 3 (Fall 2008): 369–88.

Kazan, Elia. "About Broadway and the Herring Catch." *New York Times,* October 16, 1949.

———. *Elia Kazan: A Life.* New York: Alfred A. Knopf, 1988.

———. The Elia Kazan Collection. Wesleyan Cinema Archive. Wesleyan University, Middletown, Conn.

King, W. D. "'The Shadow of a Mesmerizer': The Female Body on the 'Dark' Stage." *Theatre Journal* 49, no. 2 (May 1997): 189–206.

Knee, Adam, and Charles Musser. "William Greaves, Documentary Film-making, and the African-American Experience." *Film Quarterly* 45, no. 3 (1992): 13–25.

Kouvaros, George. *Famous Faces Not Yet Themselves: The Misfits and Icons of Postwar America*. Minneapolis: University of Minnesota Press, 2010.

Krasner, David. "I Hate Strasberg." In *Method Acting Reconsidered*, edited by David Krasner. New York: St. Martin's, 2000.

———, ed. *Method Acting Reconsidered: Theory, Practice, Future*. New York: St. Martin's Press, 2000.

Kurnick, David. *Empty Houses: Theatrical Failure and the Novel*. Princeton, N.J.: Princeton University Press, 2012.

Lavery, Carl. "Reading *The Blacks* through the 1956 Preface." *In Jean Genet: Performance and Politics*, edited by Clare Finburgh, Carl Lavery, and Maria Shevtsova. London: Palgrave Macmillan, 2006.

Leaming, Barbara. *Marilyn Monroe*. New York: Random House, 1998.

Lehmann, Hans-Thies. *Postdramatic Theatre*. Translated by Karen Jürs-Munby. London: Routledge, 2006.

Lewis, Robert. *Method—or Madness?* New York: Samuel French, 1958.

Leys, Ruth. "Mead's Voices: Imitation as Foundation, or, The Struggle against Mimesis." *Critical Inquiry* 19, no. 2 (Winter 1993): 277–307.

———. *Trauma: A Genealogy*. Chicago: University of Chicago Press, 2000.

Litvak, Joseph. *The Un-Americans: Jews, the Blacklist, and Stoolpigeon Culture*. Durham, N.C.: Duke University Press, 2009.

Macdonald, Scott. *A Critical Cinema 3: Interviews with Independent Filmmakers*. Berkeley: University of California Press, 1998.

———. *Screen Writings: Scripts and Texts by Independent Filmmakers*. Berkeley: University of California Press, 1995.

Mailer, Norman. "Theatre: The Blacks." *Village Voice*, May 11, 1961, 9.

———. *The White Negro: Superficial Reflections on the Hipster*. San Francisco: City Lights Books, 1957.

Makari, George. *Revolution in Mind: The Creation of Psychoanalysis*. New York: HarperCollins, 2008.

*Making the Misfits*. Directed by Gail Levin. DVD. Arlington, Va.: PBS Great Performances, 2002.

Malague, Rosemary. *An Actress Prepares: Women and "the Method."* New York: Routledge, 2012.

Malburne, Meredith M. "No Blues for Mister Henry: Locating Richard's Revolution." In *Reading Contemporary African American Drama: Fragments of History, Fragments of Self*, edited by Trudier Harris. New York: Peter Lang, 2007.

Marcuse, Herbert. *Eros and Civilization: A Philosophical Inquiry into Freud*. Boston: Beacon Press, 1955.

McConachie, Bruce. *American Theater in the Culture of the Cold War: Producing and Contesting Containment, 1947–1962*. Iowa City: University of Iowa Press, 2003.

———. "Method Acting and the Cold War." *Theatre Survey* 41, no. 1 (2000): 47–67.

Meisner, Sanford, and Dennis Longwell. *Sanford Meisner on Acting*. New York: Vintage, 1987.

*The Misfits*. Directed by John Huston. DVD. 1961; Santa Monica, Calif.: MGM Home Entertainment, 2001.

*The Modern Monologue: Women*. New York: Routledge, 1993.

Moi, Toril. *Ibsen and the Birth of Modernism*. Oxford: Oxford University Press, 2006.

Moreno, J. L. *Psychodrama (First Volume)*. Boston: Beacon House, 1946.

Mufti, Aamir R. "The Aura of Authenticity." *Social Text* 64 (Autumn 2000): 87–103.

*My Week with Marilyn*. Directed by Simon Curtis. DVD. London: Trademark Films, 2011.

Nadel, Alan. *Containment Culture: American Narratives, Postmodernism, and the Atomic Age*. Durham, N.C.: Duke University Press, 1995.

New Republic. "Across the Great Divide." *New Republic*, February 20, 1961.

Nicholas, Serge, Yannick Gounden, and Zachary Levine. "The Memory of Two Great Mental Calculators: Charcot and Binet's Neglected 1893 Experiments." *American Journal of Psychology* 124, no. 2 (Summer 2011): 235–42.

Ohi, Kevin. "Devouring Creation: Cannibalism, Sodomy and the Scene of Analysis in *Suddenly, Last Summer*." *Cinema Journal* 38, no. 3 (1999): 27–49.

O'Malley, Suzanne. "Can the Method Survive the Madness?" *New York Times*, October 7, 1979.

Paller, Michael. *Gentlemen Callers: Tennessee Williams, Homosexuality, and Twentieth-Century Drama*. New York: Palgrave Macmillan, 2005.

Patton, Cindy. *Cinematic Identity: Anatomy of a Problem Film*. Minneapolis: University of Minnesota Press, 2007.

Perucci, Tony. "The Red Mask of Sanity." *TDR: The Drama Review* 53, no. 4 (Winter 2009): 18–48.

Pfister, Joel. *Staging Depth: Eugene O'Neill and the Politics of Psychological Discourse*. Chapel Hill: University of North Carolina Press, 1995.

Pierpont, Claudia Roth. "Method Man." *New Yorker*, October 27, 2008.

Pitches, Jonathan. *Science and the Stanislavsky Tradition of Acting*. London: Routledge, 2006.

Puchner, Martin. *The Drama of Ideas*. Oxford: Oxford University Press, 2010.

———. *Stage Fright: Modernism, Antitheatricality, and Drama*. Baltimore: Johns Hopkins University Press, 2002.

Puzo, Mario. "Tell Me How Long the Train's Been Gone." *New York Times*, June 23, 1968. http://www.nytimes.com/books/98/03/29/specials/baldwin-tell.html.

Rancière, Jacques. *The Emancipated Spectator*. New York: Verso, 2009.

Ribot, Théodule. *Diseases of Memory: An Essay in the Positive Psychology*. Translator unknown. London: Kegan Paul, Trench and Co., 1882. Ebook.

———. *The Psychology of the Emotions*. Translator unknown. London: Walter Scott Ltd., 1897. Ebook.

Richards, Graham. *"Race," Racism and Psychology*. London: Routledge, 1997.

Roach, Joseph. *Cities of the Dead: Circum-Atlantic Performance*. New York: Columbia University Press, 1996.

———. *The Player's Passion: Studies in the Science of Acting* (Cranbury, N.J.: Associated University Presses, 1985).

Robinson, Marc. *The American Play 1787–2000*. New Haven, Conn.: Yale University Press, 2009.

Rogin, Michael. *Blackface, White Noise: Jewish Immigrants in the Hollywood Melting Pot*. Berkeley: University of California Press, 1998.

Rogoff, Gordon. "Lee Strasberg: Burning Ice." *Tulane Drama Review* 9, no. 2 (Winter 1964): 131–54.

Rose, Jacqueline. "A Rumbling of Things Unknown." *London Review of Books* 34, no. 8 (April 26, 2012): 29–34.

Ross, Andrew. *No Respect: Intellectuals and Popular Culture.* New York: Routledge, 1989.

Roth, Philip. "Channel X: Two Plays on the Race Conflict." *New York Review of Books*, May 28, 1964. 2891/articles/archives/1964/may/28/channel-x-two -plays-on-the-race-conflict/?pagination=false.

Sarris, Andrew. *The American Cinema: Directors and Directions, 1929–1968.* 1968; New York: Da Capo, 1996.

Savran, David. *Communists, Cowboys, and Queers: The Politics of Masculinity in the Work of Arthur Miller and Tennessee Williams.* Minneapolis: University of Minnesota Press, 1992.

Schechner, Richard. *The End of Humanism: Writings on Performance.* New York: Performing Arts Journal Publications, 1982.

———. *Performance Theory.* New York: Routledge, 2003.

———. "Twilight of the Gods." *Tulane Drama Review* 9, no. 2 (Winter 1964): 15–17.

Scheeder, Louis. "Strasberg's Method and the Ascendancy of American Acting." In *Training of the American Actor*, edited by Arthur Bartow. New York: Theater Communications Group, 2006.

Schneider, Rebecca. *Performing Remains: Art and War in Times of Theatrical Reenactment.* New York: Routledge, 2011.

Schnog, Nancy. "On Inventing the Psychological." In *Inventing the Psychological: Towards a Cultural History of Emotional Life in America*, edited by Nancy Schnog and Joel Pfister. New Haven, Conn.: Yale University Press, 1997.

Sedgwick, Eve Kosofsky. *Epistemology of the Closet.* Berkeley: University of California Press, 1990.

———. *Touching Feeling: Affect, Pedagogy, Performativity.* Durham, N.C.: Duke University Press, 2003.

*Shadows.* Directed by John Cassavetes. DVD. 1959; New York: Criterion Collection, 2009.

Siegel, Janice. "Tennessee Williams's *Suddenly Last Summer* and Euripedes's *Bacchae*." *International Journal of the Classical Tradition* 11, no. 4 (2005): 538–70.

Sievers, W. David. *Freud on Broadway.* New York: American Book–Stratford Press, 1955.

Sinfield, Alan. *Out on Stage: Lesbian and Gay Theater in the Twentieth-Century.* Bath, U.K.: Bath Press, 1999.

Sontag, Susan. *Against Interpretation.* New York: Farrar, Straus and Giroux, 1966.

Spielberg, Steven, Barack Obama, and Tracy Morgan. "President Obama Plays Daniel Day Lewis in White House Skit-video." *Guardian*, April 28, 2013. www.theguardian.com/world/video/2013/apr/28/president-obama-plays -daniel-day-lewis-video.

Stanislavski [Stanislavsky], Constantin. *An Actor Prepares.* Translated by Elizabeth Reynolds Hapgood. New York: Theater Arts Books, 1936.

———. *An Actor's Work.* Translated by Jean Benedetti. New York: Routledge, 2009.

———. *Creating a Role*. Translated by Elizabeth Reynolds Hapgood. New York: Routledge, 1961.

———. *Stanislavski's Legacy*. Translated by Elizabeth Reynolds Hapgood. New York: Routledge, 1999.

Strasberg, Lee. *A Dream of Passion*. Boston: Little, Brown, 1987.

———. *The Lee Strasberg Notes*. Edited by Lola Cohen. New York: Routledge, 2010.

———. *Strasberg at the Actors Studio*. Edited by Robert H. Hethmon. New York: Viking, 1965.

Strasberg, Lee, Gordon Rogoff, and Paul Gray. "Strasberg vs. TDR." *Tulane Drama Review* 11, no. 1 (Autumn 1966): 234–42.

Sturken, Marita. *Tangled Memories: The Vietnam War, the AIDS Epidemic, and the Politics of Remembering*. Berkeley: University of California Press, 1997.

*Symbiopsychotaxiplasm Take One*. Directed by William Greaves. DVD. 1968; New York: Criterion Collection, 2006.

Taubman, Howard. "Theater: 'Blues for Mister Charlie.'" *New York Times*, April 24, 1964. www.nytimes.com/books/98/03/29/specials/baldwin-charlie.html.

———. "The Blacks." *New York Times*, May 5, 1961.

Torn, Jon Leon. "A Dangerous Method: The Art of Authenticity as a Social Imperative." *Liminalities: A Journal of Performance Studies* 7, no. 4 (December 2011): 1–7.

Tyrell, John. *The Living Theatre: Art, Exile, and Outrage*. New York: Grove Press, 1995.

Warrick, John. "The Blacks and Its Impact on African American Theater." In *Jean Genet: Performance and Politics*, edited by Clare Finburgh, Carl Lavery, and Maria Shevtsova. London: Palgrave Macmillan, 2006.

Weber, Samuel. *Theatricality as Medium*. New York: Fordham University Press, 2004.

White, Edmund. *Genet: A Biography*. New York: Vintage Books, 1993.

Whyman, Rose. *The Stanislavsky System of Acting*. Cambridge: Cambridge University Press, 2008.

Wiles, David. "Burdens of Representation." In *Method Acting Reconsidered*, edited by David Krasner. New York: St. Martin's, 2000.

Williams, Tennessee. Foreword to *The Theatre of Tennessee Williams*, vol. 4. New York: New Directions, 1972.

———. *The Idea of the Actor: Drama and the Ethics of Performance*. Princeton, N.J.: Princeton University Press, 1984.

———. *Memoirs*. New York: New Directions, 1972.

———. "Notebooks." *Paris Review* 176 (2006): 131.

———. *A Streetcar Named Desire*. New York: New Directions, 1947.

———. "Suddenly Last Summer." In *The Theatre of Tennessee Williams*, vol. 3. New York: New Directions, 1972.

———. MS Thr 397, Harvard Theatre Collection, Houghton Library, Cambridge.

Worthen, William B. "Stanislavsky and the Ethos of Acting." *Theatre Journal* 35, no. 1 (1983): 32–40.

———. *The Idea of the Actor: Drama and the Ethics of Performance*. Princeton, N.J.: Princeton University Press, 1984.

Zolotow, Maurice. "The Stars Rise Here." *Saturday Evening Post*, May 18, 1957.

# INDEX

abstract expressionism, 103
*Acting: The First Six Lessons* (Boleslavsky).
 *See* Boleslavsky, Richard
Actors Studio: audio recordings of, 10–11,
 40, 43, 56, 108; Baldwin's experience
 at, 17, 72–75, 83–84, 92; criticism of,
 17, 26–27, 65–68, 72–75, 83–84, 98,
 119–20, 137n6; Don Fellows, membership 112–13; Eli Wallach, membership,
 25; Elia Kazan, founding of and work
 at, 16, 33, 49, 68, 73, 107; Marilyn
 Monroe at, 26–27; mythology of, 105–
 6; *Strasberg at the Actors Studio: The
 Tape-Recorded Sessions*, 10–11, 40;
 Strasberg's work at, 10–11, 26–27, 40–
 44, 54, 56, 83–84, 98, 121–22; text,
 attitude toward, 108; William Greaves's
 membership in, 17, 104; Williams's relationship to, 16, 49, 54, 56
actressing, 49
Adler, Stella, 9–10, 44, 67, 99, 124n24,
 128n11
Adorno, Theodor, 106–7; *The Jargon of
 Authenticity*, 106
affect: affect theory, 21; affective memory
 exercise, 14, 36–38, 129n21; and performance, 19, 111–12, 117, 118. *See also*
 emotional memory
African American: artists and writers, 17,
 100; realism, 134n33; representation of,
 69, 80, 104; theater, 100, 134n33; universalism, critiques of, 15
Albee, Edward, 73, 74, 114, 130n1; *Who's
 Afraid of Virginia Woolf?*, 114–15
American: acting, 10, 11, 12, 17, 27, 74,
 80, 86, 98; adoption of Stanislavsky,
 8–9, 17; artists, 11, 103, 104, 116;
 authenticity, 4–5, 105–6; context for
 Genet, 94; history, 4, 11, 100; identity,
 65–69, 77, 86, 98–99, 100, 104–6;
 morality, 47–48; nationalism, 65–67;
 normativity, 111, 114; performance of
 Americanness, 4, 68–69; psychology
 and psychoanalysis, 39, 76–77; realist

theater, 73–74, 86, 92; superiority, 65–
 67; universalism, 15, 100
American Laboratory Theatre, 9
Angelou, Maya, 91–92
anticommunism, 66–68
antisemitism, 26–27, 68, 120
Antoine, Andre, 8
Artaud, Antonin, 13
aura, 107. *See also* Benjamin, Walter
Aurobindo, Sri, 117, 121
authenticity: in acting, 50, 105, 107–8,
 137n6; in Benjamin's "The Work of Art
 in the Age of Mechanical Reproduction," 107; in Cold War discourse, 114;
 emotional, 18; *The Jargon of Authenticity*, 106–7; and mediation, 113, 119,
 121, 137n6; in Method discourse, 50,
 106, 108; in New Left discourse, 105–
 7; in Obama's video, 5; *The Politics of
 Authenticity*, 105; and theater, 17–18,
 104–8; in *Where's Daddy?*, 107–8
avant-garde: anti-textual performance, 11,
 13, 15, 103, 104, 108; commonalities
 with Method acting, 104, 117; Method
 acting, opposed to 7, 11, 17, 22, 92,
 98–99, 103, 108

*Bacchae*, 51
Baker, Carroll, 27
Baldwin, James: at the Actors Studio, 17,
 72–76; *Another Country*, 87, 134n39;
 *Blues for Mister Charlie*, 15–17, 19, 69,
 73–87, 89–90, 91–92, 96, 98, 134n39;
 and Elia Kazan, 73–74; and Genet, 91–
 92; *Giovanni's Room*, 72; Method acting,
 critique of 69, 73, 81–83, 85–87; novelization of theater, 13; politics, 74–75,
 80, 84, 89, 91; psychology, critique of,
 77–78, 83; and Stanislavsky, 87, 88–89;
 and Strasberg, 84; *Tell Me How Long the
 Train's Been Gone*, 17, 71–73, 84, 86–87,
 89, 133n7; "Theater: The Negro In and
 Out," 74; theories of acting, 19, 75–76,
 79–80; universalism, critique of, 89, 118

*151*

universalism: American ideology of, 11, 15,
    100; in Method acting, 4, 11, 13, 15,
    69, 73, 76, 81, 84–85, 89–90, 96, 100

Vakhtangov, Evgeni, 10–11, 130n39
Vidal, Gore, 59, 131n17
*Village Voice*, 93–94

Wallach, Eli, 25
Weber, Samuel, 100
*Where's Daddy?* (Inge). *See* Inge, William
White, Edmund, 91
White House Correspondents' Dinner, 3,
    68–69
*Who's Afraid of Virginia Woolf?* (Albee).
    *See* Albee, Edward
Williams, Tennessee: acting, theories of,
    19, 48–49; Actors Studio, connection
    to, 16–17; advice about translation of
    *The Blacks*, 91; camp, 48–49; challenge

to psychological realism, 16, 50, 59–60;
    Inge's allusion in *Where's Daddy?*, 108,
    138n23; Mailer's homophobic critique,
    94; melodrama, 49, 60; as Method
    playwright, 16–17, 48–49; psycho-
    analysis, 47–48, 50–55, 58 131n5; as
    representative midcentury playwright,
    12, 117; sexuality, 15–16, 19, 48, 50,
    55–60, 130n1, 131n29
    WORKS: *The Glass Menagerie*, 49; *A
    Streetcar Named Desire*, 16, 48–49,
    109–10; *Suddenly Last Summer*, 15,
    17, 47–60, 131n17, 138n23; *Sweet
    Bird of Youth*, 17, 48, 72. See also
    *Suddenly Last Summer*
Wordsworth, William, 38
World War I, 45
World War II, 5, 76–77

Yiddish, 26, 67–68. *See also* Jewishness